PRAISE THE LORD...
& PASS THE LEECHES

PRAISE THE LORD...
& PASS THE LEECHES

*Stories that reveal one
man's passion for fishing & hunting,
allowing God to speak through
means otherwise un-noticed.*

by

DEN PLUIMER
foreword by Al Lindner

TATE PUBLISHING *& Enterprises*

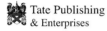
Tate Publishing
& Enterprises

DEDICATION

I could not write without inspiration, and my immediate family is instrumental in providing that motivation. Our daughter Joy has always encouraged me, challenged me, and urged me to "preach the Gospel" any way I can. With sons Mike and Mark, I've spent innumerable days on a lake, in a slough, or in the woods, and I treasure every one of those days. Many of those times are chronicled in this book. My son-in-law, Chad, and two daughters-in-law, Heather and Laurie, continue to bless me through the way they are living their lives in obedience to the Lord and through their appreciation of and curiosity about the wildlife around them. I wish to dedicate this book to them out of my gratitude for their support.

All the ideas, memories, and lessons brought to life in these pages, however, would be nothing more than dreams were it not for my wife Sheri. She has always been my encourager, has always urged me to keep thinking, keep jotting down my thoughts, keep creating. She has been my strongest supporter. But more importantly, she is still my closest friend. And never has she made me feel guilty for spending so much time on the water, in the woods, or in the slough. For that I am indebted.

In addition, I wish to dedicate this book to my three grand-children, Mikey, 7, Meikea, 7, and Maddie, 4. They are yet too young to realize what it means to dedicate, but my prayer for them is twofold: that as adults, they may love the Lord with the enthusiasm they show today, and that they may find as much joy and pleasure outdoors as I have in my life.

I also want to credit Terry Kragt, a frequent companion in my boat, a man who is passionate not only about fish and game, but also family. Grandchildren are at the center of his life.

Finally, I wish to dedicate this book to four gentlemen with whom I've been privileged to share so many experiences: Mike Reitsma, Ron Bouma, Jeff Poppema, and Daryl Marcus. We have huddled together in a duck blind, we've tramped the sloughs for pheasants, we've pounded the waves together while jigging for walleyes. And we've gone to our knees in prayer many times. All men should be so fortunate as I to have family and friends such as all of these.

TABLE OF CONTENTS

FOREWORD

Most folks probably go fishing much like I go bowling. For me, it's something to do, a diversion. I pursue it for a short period of time when it's convenient, and then forget about it until the next opportunity arises.

On the other hand, fishing, for me, is a "lifestyle." Not only is it my source of income, it's my passion. I subscribe to and read countless magazines about fishing. I watch TV shows about fishing. I surf internet sites about fishing. I fish in tournaments. I give seminars about fishing, and even used to be a fishing guide. In fact, most of my close friends are also "lifestyle" fishermen.

It makes perfect sense, then, that since fishing or fishing-related activities take up the bulk of my time, that this is one of the ways through which God relates to and communicates with me.

Denny Pluimer, acknowledged by his peers as a successful high school biology teacher, is also a "lifestyle" outdoors person. In other words, for him, fishing and hunting are much more than hobbies. His life—much like mine—revolves around the fishing aspects of the out-of-doors.

Being from Minnesota, I intimately recognize many of the places and activities named in this book. Thus I can actually feel and experience the emotion of the events that Denny and his friends are experiencing. But one doesn't have to hail from Minnesota to appreciate what is unfolding upon the pages. You don't even have to be an "up North" fisherman, nor even a committed Christian, for that matter—although that is to be hoped for.

The episodes related in this book are taken from Denny's life and illustrate how the God of creation touches and interacts with him in the most exciting, as well as the most mundane, of everyday events. It is good to know that the Creator is always watching out for us, no matter which way or how hard the wind blows or how high the waves become.

"Praise the Lord and Pass the Leeches" might not have the same impact as "Praise the Lord and Pass the Crickets" might have on a Southern bream fisherman, or that "Praise the Lord and Pass the Sand Fleas" might have on a coastal surf angler. But the point is clear enough: same God, different places. And, of course, people are people, no matter which species they fish for. So it makes no difference where you live—or what you do. While fishermen have a lot of opportunity to see God's handiwork in natural events, I am equally sure that there are many other "lifestyles" where God is just as evident. In the world of medicine, for example, His miracles are surely evident every day.

Yet in all cases God gives people the opportunities to live out the Gospel in their daily lives, no matter what calling they follow. And that's what this book is about: living out the Gospel in daily living—in this case, the life of a fisherman.

AL LINDNER

PREFACE

A wood-duck sailing in with cupped wings . . .
A black Lab rigid on point at cornfield's edge . . .
A ruffed grouse bursting from a soggy tag-alder thicket . . .
Shedding cattails silhouetted against a fuchsia sky . . .
The pre-dawn quackings and stirrings from an October marsh . . .
Waves lapping against a boat transom during a walleye drift . . .
The unmistakable "thunk" of a largemouth bass inhaling a plastic worm . . .
The pungent lingering odor of Hoppe's #9 in the den after a day's hunt.

All of these sensations are part of the images, scents, and sounds of the sporting life. To some folks, they mean nothing; to others they represent a fleeting fancy. But to some of us, they are part of the fabric of life itself. To experience them, to participate, to partake, is to live. When such experiences from nature's bountiful storehouse also serve to reveal lessons about our Creator's ingenuity, creativity, and diversity, then a sportsperson has truly participated in the "abundant life."

This book is an attempt to relate a life-long love affair with all things wild and free and to demonstrate how such pursuits as hunting and fishing can draw a person into a deeper, closer walk with God. With that in mind, may your livewell always be brimming, and may your game-bag always be bulging.

PRAISE THE LORD . . . AND PASS THE LEECHES

June, 1975. Moses Bar, an expansive reef on one of Minnesota's true jewels—a 70,000-acre windswept lake the state map labels as "Winnibigoshish." But to thousands of walleye anglers, she is fondly known as "Big Winnie." The name is often uttered in tones approaching reverence, for Winnie is indeed a rare jewel; her natural spawning grounds produce prodigious numbers of walleyes every spring—and many of them become willing, even eager to inhale an angler's offering of leech, crawler, or shiner.

I was sharing a boat that day with my close friend, Pastor Mike Reitsma. Even though that was decades ago, I can still hear the metallic sound of waves lapping against the transom of our aluminum boat as we precisely backtrolled the edges of the bar, the Lowrance flasher reading depths of 18' to 30', depending on how well Mike could maneuver the boat along the steep drop-off.

We were running "Lindy rigs," live bait rigs absolutely genius in their simplicity and deadly on all species of game fish when tipped with the appropriate live bait. On this particular day, that bait was leeches . . . jumbo leeches, black and slippery and very lively. A southwest breeze provided the classic "walleye chop" we hear so much about as we backtrolled Moses, and for awhile that morning, the walleyes were concentrated on the upper ledge, still recuperating from the rigors of spawning. The abundant forage of summer had not yet appeared; and the walleyes were hungry, and they wanted our leeches! It seemed as though every few minutes one of us would feel that unmistakable gentle tightening of the line as the sliding sinker bumped along the sand bottom—a walleye pickup! We would give line for a couple seconds, close the reel's bail, and reel up the slack line, then set the hook. Invariably, the hook-set would be met with substantial weight and the steady pulsing resistance of a walleye.

And so it went, at least for a couple hours. The fish were on, and so were we. I can still see Pastor Mike sitting there in the back of the boat, eyes glued on the depth finder, while that silly, wrinkled, dirty old orange fishing cap sat askew on his head. He was totally enthralled with our good fortune, and all of the sudden he grinned, looked me in the eye, and loudly announced, "Praise the Lord, Den . . . and pass the leeches!"

That simple phrase, incongruous as it may seem, became a defining moment in my life. I had been raised in a truly Christian home, with loving and caring parents. Religion was not superficial, and I was raised to live in obedience to God. But all of the sudden, my close friend Mike, in one short quip, manifested what it meant to integrate one's Christianity with his daily life. I guess it had never occurred to me that not only was it appropriate for a Christian to have great fun, but God also provided it, and He loved to hear His people praising Him for the fun they were having!

What a blessing it is to enjoy life, to be excited about living, to be able to have fun. But a deeper dimension is added if we realize that God is responsible for our everyday joys; remember, He is the giver of all good gifts. Daily activities can bring great joy; they can also remind us of our loving Creator's goodness, and that is what this book is all about. Millions of us men and women enjoy the outdoors—hunting, fishing, camping, hiking. This book attempts to take us all one step further, to meet God in the outdoors and worship Him there.

"So . . . Praise the Lord . . . and pass those leeches!"

Philemon 4–7:

I always thank my God as I remember you in my prayers, because I hear about your faith in the Lord Jesus and your love for all the saints. I pray that you may be active in sharing your faith, so that you will have a full understanding of every good thing we have in Christ. Your love has given me great joy and encouragement, because you, brother, have refreshed the hearts of the saints.

CATTAIL CATHEDRAL

I am of the opinion that every hunt is a good hunt. Middle age may tend to foster that notion, because at the back of my mind lurks the probing question of how many more days afield I may have. The Lord teaches us that our days are numbered, but we don't all share the same number. I don't sense any morbidity in this thinking, but rather an urgency to make the absolute most of every hunt.

Nevertheless, there are good hunts and there are great hunts. And then there are unforgettable hunts. Such was the case on October 12, 1997. My son Mark was pursuing a biology degree at a small college three hours from home. Dordt College was chosen partly because of its mark as an excellent Christian college with a reputation for turning out good teachers, but also because of its proximity to our home in central Minnesota. For Mark, that meant that autumn weekends could easily be spent chasing ducks, pheasants, and grouse with me. Dordt College also happens to be situated in prime farmland resplendent with corn, soybeans, and ringnecks. Some college students fritter away their parents' tuition money on parties and wild times; my wife and I had no such worries about Mark. But when he scheduled his fall classes so that he could spend afternoons chasing pheasants, we saw where his priorities really were!

On this weekend, Mark had come home for some local duck hunting with his older brother, Mike, and me. The three of us had enjoyed a Saturday duck hunt in the slough just two miles down the road from home. We also sneaked out to the slough for 45 minutes before church on Sunday morning. By mid-afternoon, Mike had packed up and begun the two hour trip to his home. Mark was getting ready to head back to college; after all, there *is* studying to be done. Sheri and I were planning on attending the evening service at church.

Mark seemed in no hurry to leave; the dorm held no particular appeal, and the afternoon was beautiful . . . and lingering. As Mark carried another armload of gear to his truck, he paused, looked me in the face, and I knew what he was thinking—*"Let's spend the sunset in the slough."* Forget the trip back to college; Mark could leave early in the morning if need be. Forget church—now that concept was markedly more radical. I'm sure in my long life I have "skipped" church a time or two. But never, ever to go hunting! With my upbringing, that was tantamount to heresy, and even now I don't flaunt this decision, but at that time there was no hesitation—father and son needed this special time together in the slough at sundown.

The strange thing is I don't remember the quantitative details of that evening hunt. I can consult my log book to find out, but I have no recollection how many ducks came in, how many shots we took or whether we bagged two, three, or ten ducks, or none at all. But I vividly remember the setting. Mark and I shared a personal worship experience that evening. The two of us stood in waist-deep water—the pungent odor of swamp gas around us, the sound of coots clucking among the duckweed, tan cattails on every side—while in the western sky the sun dropped, leaving the most dazzling array of colors either of us had ever witnessed.

We weren't in "church," because God's church is really His people, and Mark and I were alone in that slough. But we were not alone. Creator God Himself was there with us, along with a multitude of His creatures, from dragonflies and water striders to muskrats, coots, and ducks. The most gorgeous stained-glass windows of the world's most beautiful cathedral are only a faint facsimile of that sunset. I saw Mark silhouetted next to a muskrat mound—duck call swinging from his neck, his Browning BPS resting over his shoulder—gazing over the still cattails into the western sky, oblivious to any ducks that may have been dropping into the swamp for their night-time rest.

I wasn't in church, but I was worshipping my Heavenly Father with a deeper reverence than I have during all but the most sacred traditional worship services. And God reached down and touched me there in the slough. I sensed that He created that sunset just for me, for my pure pleasure. We met there in the slough that evening—God and I—and my eyes grew moist as He gently reminded me again how blessed I am, how good life is.

Ever since that night, I find myself looking for another "cattail cathedral." I'm sure one day I will find one; after all, God creates them all the time. But I doubt I'll find one this special.

Psalm 19:1–6:

The heavens declare the glory of God; the skies proclaim the work of his hands. Day after day they pour forth speech; night after night they display knowledge.

There is no speech or language where their voice is not heard. Their voice goes out into all the earth, their words to the ends of the world.

In the heavens he has pitched a tent for the sun, which is like a bridegroom coming forth from his pavilion, like a champion rejoicing to run his course. It rises at one end of the heavens and makes its circuit to the other; nothing is hidden from its heat.

THE PEREGRINE

May 15, 1999—perhaps an insignificant date to most people, but there is a group of about one million Minnesotans who, if pressed, could reflect a few minutes and recall, *"Oh, yeah, the walleye opener!"* Few events in the calendar year spark as much anticipation, enthusiasm and fever as this single annual tradition.

The opener of '99 was a traditional one for me also—I was fishing my favorite walleye lake, Big Winnie, with my long-time fishing and hunting companion, Ron Bouma, and his son Troy. Neither of my sons were available this time; Mike's wife Heather had just days before given birth to their firstborn, while Mark was 700 miles away at seminary.

Early afternoon found us out in Bowens Flats, just outside Cutfoot Sioux. Action had been steady, we had released several fish, and we had many decent "eaters" swimming in the livewell. Under a heavily overcast sky, with a moderate southeast breeze creating the perfect "walleye chop," we were engaged in a long drift over the shallow sand and rubble bottom of Winnie's north shore. Methodically, we pumped our shiner minnows and chartreuse jigheads off the lake bottom, waiting for that unmistakable "pickup" of a hungry passing walleye.

Suddenly, something caught the corner of my eye, and I glanced skyward. Scarcely 50 yards from my boat, a peregrine falcon had folded its wings and begun a power dive from 100 yards in the air. I watched as it streaked—yes streaked—toward the lake's surface. Informed sources document the peregrine's diving speed at 200 mph!

I remember wondering what the falcon was doing. Unlike two other common predators over Winnie, the osprey and bald eagle, a peregrine falcon does not often hunt for fish. Rather, the peregrine's taste is for birds, and he is a superb hunter. We were almost a mile from shore; no songbirds would be way out here. And then I saw it—a blue jay winging its way toward us.

Directly in front of us unfolded the most spectacular, most awesome chase scene I'd ever witnessed. The typical police chase scene on any cop video is a lullaby in comparison. Like a missile, the grey peregrine fell, but there was no sudden "puff" of feathers; for at the last instant the blue jay side-stepped, and the falcon's talons missed their mark. For almost 30 seconds, the two avian participants waged battle over our boat. The peregrine would quickly climb, then suddenly tilt into a nosedive. Incredibly, the jay was able to thwart the falcon's every attempt, first zigging, then zagging, frantically fighting for survival. Reaching the safety of the shoreline looked like an impossibility, and the poor jay seemed doomed. It appeared certain that one bird would fulfill its God-created destiny as a mighty hunter, while the other would ultimately serve as fertilizer for some woodland wildflowers next spring.

But then came an incredible, mind-blowing turn of events: out of sheer terror, and literally fighting for its life, the harassed jay turned toward my boat, and with the peregrine poised for another dive, he came in for a landing. One lone, very desperate blue jay, in a last-ditch effort, placed its fate into the hands of three fishermen rather than take its chance any longer against the persistent falcon.

We all sat stunned and stared in disbelief. Had this actually happened? Did this bird willingly choose to perch in our boat, scarcely two feet from our grasp? For a full minute, the jay sat there, shaking and trembling, beak agape in terror, until Troy spoke up.

"You think I can catch him?"

He reached out his hand to grasp the blue jay, but that was too much. With Troy's fingers scarcely inches away, the bird lifted off the boat. The still circling falcon made another swoop, but incredibly, missed again! The jay flew only 50 feet to the next boat and promptly landed in *it*. Those fishermen were just as awestruck as we had been when it landed by us, and the refugee stayed with them for a full three or four minutes until the peregrine grew impatient and left. Then and only then did the blue jay opt for the safety of the shore, while all us fishermen were left staring and shaking our heads, still dazed at what we'd witnessed.

I've re-lived that scene many times since that day, wondering what actually transpired out there on Big Winnie. Many lessons can likely be drawn from the experience, but one stands out for me. No matter how gloomy or hopeless a situation seems to be, we are not lost. God can provide a way out, a safe haven even in the most desperate of situations. Maybe sometimes we, like the blue jay, must take a huge leap of faith. God is an ever-present help in times of trouble. Nothing, absolutely nothing, is too big for Him to handle. Not even a diving peregrine.

Isaiah 40: 28–31:

Do you not know? Have you not heard? The Lord is the everlasting God, the Creator of the ends of the earth. He will not grow tired or weary, and his understanding no one can fathom. He gives strength to the weary and increases the power of the weak. Even youths grow tired and weary and young men stumble and fall; but those who hope in the Lord will renew their strength. They will soar on wings like eagles; they will run and not grow weary, they will walk and not be faint.

LOVE LIFTED ME

About 8:30 one Saturday morning in December, Mike and Mark and I were driving through Sioux County, Iowa on a late season pheasant hunt. We were heading for a favorite waterway when two roosters flew across the road in front of the truck and sailed out into a large patch of tall grass about a quarter mile off the road. Instantly abandoning our initial plan, we determined then and there to look those two fellows up. I braked, turned into the first driveway, and pulled up to the farmhouse, where Mike got out to ask permission to hunt.

We interrupted a pleasant farmer and his wife from their breakfast, but the gentleman quickly granted us permission, cautioning us not to shoot toward the barn. Mike thanked him, and we parked the truck, let our black Lab, Lexus, out of her kennel, and loaded our guns. Hearts pounding in anticipation, we strode across the bean field toward the grass. Upon reaching it, we observed that it was not a huge tract of grass after all, but rather a square sewage lagoon, totally surrounded by a wide strip of grass that was at least chest high. This was beautiful cover; it just looked "birdy," and at present, it held at least two roosters.

In spite of the bright sunshine, the air temperature was cold, and we observed that the lagoon was totally frozen over. Since it was such a big pond—around 75 yards across—the three of us decided to split up to cover the grass adequately. Mark and Lexus headed east while Mike and I walked south around the western edge. Slowly and methodically, since we were without a dog, Mike and I wove our way through the cover, and after we had walked only 50 yards, a gaudy rooster erupted noisily just ahead of Mike. He swung on the bird, touched off a shot, and the rooster folded in a cloud of feathers. By this time, Mark and Lexus were on the opposite side of the lagoon, but when Lexus heard Mike's shot, she bolted toward us, hitting the ice at full throttle. She reached the middle of the lagoon, when all of the sudden the sheet ice gave way underneath her, and she plunged headfirst into the frigid water. All three of us heard the splashing and subsequent yelping, and we rushed to the ice edge. Poor Lex was frantic as she vainly tried to pull herself up onto firm ice. Every time she got a grip with her front paws, the ice would further break away and she would go under again. Mike and Mark and I stood helplessly by and began to panic ourselves, not knowing whether the pond was five or fifteen feet deep, but believing that Lexus was not going to make it. Already her frantic attempts at reaching safety were beginning to sap her energy. She began to weaken. Mark was about crying as we hollered encouragement to Lexus, not daring to venture out onto the ice ourselves.

Then I remembered I had a tow rope back in the truck. I didn't know exactly how we should use it, but maybe we could somehow "lasso" Lexus, or maybe one of us would even dare head out with the rope around our waist. At any rate, I felt I had to do something, so I sprinted the quarter mile back to the truck, praying all the way that the dog wouldn't drown.

Minutes later, I was bouncing back across the field in the truck, and as I slid up to the lagoon, the scene I witnessed almost paralyzed me. Spread-eagle out on the ice, just feet from the thrashing Lexus, lay Mike, his arm extending as far out as possible as he slowly inched closer to the hole. Mark lay directly behind him, firmly grasping one of Mike's ankles with both hands. Both boys were at least 30 yards from the shore, and as we were later informed, over deep water. All I could think of was that I was about to lose a dog and both sons. It was one of the most frightening moments of my life.

Miraculously, Lex's stamina persisted until Mike's outstretched arm reached her collar. More miraculously, the thin ice underneath Mike held him and Lexus both, and Mark managed to drag them to safety. A very tense, precarious situation, in fact potentially tragic, ended with a huge sigh of relief and a prayer of profound thanksgiving. The sole lingering effect was a tired and extremely smelly black Lab.

I was so relieved to have my sons safe by my side that I simply could not reprimand them for their decision to crawl out and rescue the dog. But aloud I questioned the wisdom of that decision.

"Dad," Mike said, "Lex was drowning. She would not have lasted five more minutes. We couldn't just watch her go. Could you?" Mike and Mark willingly put their lives in peril for the safety of their dog.

God—my heavenly father—once gave His beloved and only Son up for me—to rescue me from a fate significantly worse than drowning in sewage. Just as incredulous, my heavenly father continues to "go out onto thin ice" for me on a daily basis. It seems I am constantly putting myself into a predicament that is sure to doom me. Then God rescues me once again. Sometimes it is from physical harm, through the help of a guardian angel or two. At other times it may be a rescue from some spiritual snare I've encountered. It doesn't matter; God's hand is always there to draw me up from the hole that promises to consume me.

I guess after He has invested so much in me, He is not about to sit and watch me go under.

Psalm 40:1–5:

I waited patiently for the Lord; he turned to me and heard my cry. He lifted me out of the slimy pit, out of the mud and mire; he set my feet on a rock and gave me a firm place to stand. He put a new song in my mouth, a hymn of praise to our God. Many will see and fear and put their trust in the Lord.

Blessed is the man who makes the Lord his trust, who does not look to the proud, to those who turn aside to false gods. Many, O Lord my God, are the wonders you have done. The things you planned for us no one can recount to you; were I to speak and tell of them, they would be too many to declare.

DOCK SITTING

Look closely at a detailed map of Crow Wing County, and you'll eventually see it—a 300 acre dot of blue named Clough Lake. Surely the name does not offer the same appeal as would a Bass Lake, Pike Lake, or Big Mantrap, but then Clough really *isn't* very appealing. We always called it Pluimer Lake because, after all, it was *our* lake; at least we were the only people living on it. But now a young fellow has moved in "next door," about a half mile down the shore, and he plans to erect a log home eventually. There goes the neighborhood.

Clough Lake truly is like its name: unassuming and unappealing, at least to typical folks. Though its water is clean and clear, it is weed-choked and boasts a maximum depth of eight feet. People choose to live on a lake for a variety of reasons, to fish, to swim, to boat. Yet none of these activities can be enjoyed on our lake. If Clough were a fish, it would undoubtedly be a carp; if it were a duck, it would be a spoonbill; and if it were a car, well, my guess is it would likely be a Yugo. In short, this is an undesirable lake, and its tax rate confirms that assessment.

All in all, there is nothing very special about this lake; then again, there is something very special about it. It is secluded. It is quiet. It is practically uninhabited. And it is our refuge from modernity and materialism.

One evening, I sat out on our dock to relax after supper. As I watched an osprey circle immediately overhead, all the while uttering its characteristic "chirp, chirp," a whitetail doe stepped out of the woods and into the water down the shoreline, its late summer russet coat glistening under the evening sun. Suddenly, to the south, a lone loon let loose with a short wail, then another. I knew precisely what that signaled, and I rose and scanned the sky above me until I finally spotted it—a mature bald eagle soaring above the lake, ever watching for a helpless fish or a baby loon.

I considered myself incredibly fortunate at that moment; four of my favorite species of wildlife were framed before me simultaneously! What a gift! That is precisely why my family treasures our cabin on Clough Lake.

I've never seen a jet-ski or a speed boat on it, and I can count on one hand the number of boats that venture out onto its water in a summer.

When Satan pummels me with the trials and frustrations of daily living, I can retreat to the end of the dock, pull up a chair, and simply sit awhile. Gradually the pessimism, the uneasiness, and the anxiety all slip away, replaced with a peace and tranquility only God can provide. Different people can find that peace in different surroundings, but for me it readily approaches on my dock. Maybe "dock-sitting" should be a required pastime for everyone now and then. I'll even wager that some of our country's major problems could be solved out on the end of a dock. There's no room for hostility out here.

Matthew 11:27–30:

All things have been committed to me by my Father. No one knows the Son except the Father, and no one knows the Father except the Son and those to whom the Son chooses to reveal him. Come to me, all you who are weary and burdened, and I will give you rest. Take my yoke upon you and learn from me, for I am gentle and humble in heart, and you will find rest for your souls. For my yoke is easy and my burden is light.

SOMETIMES GOD LAUGHS

We all remember an uncle or perhaps a grandfather who always seemed to have a twinkle in his eye and a grin on his face. Every time we stopped in for a visit, we knew we were in for some teasing, some joking around. His sense of humor would invariably brighten our day; you felt lighthearted when you left the place.

Well, if we are observant during our varied excursions into the outdoors, we will see that our Creator reveals a wide variety of His own attributes, one of which is a sense of humor, He wants to share with us. I think you've all seen it.

Back in my early guiding days, I was a Senior Instructor for Camp Fish, America's only full time fishing instructional school for youth. That experience put me in touch with some of America's finest anglers and also introduced me to many of the corporations comprising the fishing tackle industry. One week I was scheduled to guide a father/son group into Canada on a fly-in trip for muskies and smallmouth bass. It has always been a pleasure for me to witness fathers and sons enjoying time together, and this Canadian adventure was no exception.

I had the privilege of taking my own son Mike along on that trip, and our "duty" was to guide the other members of our group. I was in charge of four fathers and four sons. Each father and son occupied a boat, and I was to insure that all outboards were running well, that all members of the party were using appropriate safety precautions, and that everyone was finding cooperative fish. Each father basically fished alone with his son, but my task was to scout the area, pre-fish it, and be able to point out hotspots and current hot techniques. Hey, as they say, it's a dirty job, but someone has to do it!

Kay Lake, Ontario, is a typical "Canadian shield lake," oligotrophic by biological classification, characterized by deep, cold, rocky water, with dozens of shallow bays holding healthy green cabbage beds. The two species of dominance are muskies and smallmouth bass—arguably the two most impressive fighters in freshwater. Fishing presentations for muskies are totally different from those employed for smallies. Consequently, the fishing was not boring. A person could spend a couple hours pitching huge jerkbaits over the weedbeds for muskies, then when he tired he could switch over to his light spinning gear and cast tiny crankbaits or jigs. The action for both species was fairly consistent, and the fishing was just plain fun.

On the third afternoon, Mike and I cruised into a rocky, pine-rimmed bay to check on two members of our party. As we edged closer, we could see that both father and son were busy heaving musky baits over an expansive bed of healthy cabbage weeds. Both guys were making strong overhand casts with heavy baitcasting equipment, sending a visible spray of water from their reels with each cast. The lures flew out in long arcs, finally plunking into the water with a noisy splash before beginning the arduous retrieve toward the boat.

I killed the outboard and quietly coasted toward the father's boat. "How ya doin'?" I asked.

"Great," came the reply. "But, I'll tell you what . . . there's a big musky lying in shallow water and it won't even *look* at our lures!"

"Really?" I asked, his expression of "big" immediately piquing my interest. "Where is he?"

The son pointed toward an island near the far end of the bay. "It is lying in the sun right next to a big fallen tree on the other side of that island. It's easy to spot. You guys have to try for it; we can't get it to budge!"

Well, that was challenge enough. Mike and I motored toward the island. I slowly cruised around the one-acre outcrop, then turned the motor off as we approached the far side. A lone fir tree stood sentinel on the island, but another had long ago fallen into the lake, its tangled branches providing excellent cover on an otherwise clean bottom. Sure enough, even from 20 yards away, we saw her—a long, torpedo-shaped fish lying parallel to the tree's trunk. Her nose was facing away from the island, she was motionless, and as the boy had said, probably sunning herself in the cool June water. She was beautiful, and though not a true monster, we judged her to be in the 25 pound range.

In a circumstance such as this, a considerate, caring father would calmly wait and let his son make the first couple casts. I must confess a character flaw here, for I scrambled for my musky rod, equipped with a gaudy chartreuse and red tandem bucktail and immediately sent a cast hurling past the musky's head. I brought that bucktail directly in front of her nose and gave it an erratic motion. No matter. She may as well have been carved in stone. Both Mike and I made repeated casts toward her, always with the same outcome: absolutely no response.

Then, on perhaps my fourth or fifth cast, when the huge pulsating lure was only a couple feet from the fish's nose, three very chunky smallmouth bass darted up from the deeper water off the fallen tree toward my lure. The lead fish actively nipped at the billowing bucktail as I stared in disbelief.

"Did you see that?" I whispered.

"They were four pounds for sure," Mike replied excitedly. "What are they doing chasing a humongous lure like that?" We cast twice more and each time those pugnacious smallmouths came up from the rocks, swam directly in front of the musky, and chased our offerings. All of the sudden it dawned on me that if those smallies were so aggressive as to chase and nip a lure almost as long as themselves, they just may be hungry. I dropped my musky rod and picked up my light weight, six foot spinning outfit, which was rigged with Berkley Trilene 6 pound line and a two inch Rebel crawdad crankbait. The lure had been dynamite all week, enticing many smallmouths in the one to two-pound range, but nothing so big as the three we had just seen.

I flipped the miniscule crankbait out toward the fallen tree, gave the rod tip two twitches and began my retrieve. There was a silver flash and a boil on the surface as that musky catapulted onto my crankbait. A 25 pound missile with teeth snipped the little lure off my line without so much as an ounce of resistance while I stood with slack line, shaky knees, and disbelief. Thirty seconds ago, an 18 inch smallmouth bass entertained visions of swallowing my 12 inch bucktail while the musky ignored the traditional offering. Now I had thrown a fake crayfish lure at that same smallie, and the musky, who for the past hour had ignored every sensible offering, had just used my ultralight lure as an appetizer.

You figure that one out. It is not out of the question that God chose to play with my mind that day. I believe He even grinned. After all, every good father plays with his kids.

Mark 9:36–37:

He took a little child and had him stand among them. Taking him in his arms, he said to them, "Whoever welcomes one of these little children in my name welcomes me; and whoever welcomes me does not welcome me but the one who sent me.

DIVING DUCKS

It is an understatement to suggest that I am passionate about water-fowling. But in my maturing years, I am mellowing somewhat; whereas sleet, snow, and driving rain used to signal good duck hunting weather, I now find myself rather enjoying a 60 degree sunny day out in a duck blind. My son Mike, however, is still young, energetic . . . and crazy; to him, genuine duck hunting means frostbite, iced decoys, and shivering Labrador retrievers.

So it was that the second Saturday of November last year found Mike and me with a dilemma: it was the final Saturday of central Minnesota's deer season, and we had already completed our hunt the previous week, leaving us with a free Saturday in the fall (a rare commodity, just ask my wife Sheri). Not wanting to "waste" the day, we had three choices: grouse, pheasant, or duck—sort of a no-brainer according to Mike. Pheasants would be fair game for another month; grouse could be hunted another six weeks, and they were heading toward the bottom of their ten-year population cycle, anyway; but ducks . . . ah, there we go!

Minnesota's short-lived autumn was fast merging into winter, and the sloughs were already iced over. Every local duck had long departed for warmer waters, and now the divers were streaming across the state, meaning that any open water with a good cattail point could possibly serve as a duck magnet.

Lake Wagonga has built an enviable late season waterfowling reputation, and my good friend Daryl owns a secluded piece of woodland on the north bay. On that November day, he graciously offered permission for Mike and me to launch our canoe from his property, thereby gaining access to the lake for a duck hunt. Daryl's property is accessible via a one mile dirt trail winding through the woods surrounding the lake, so we loaded our canoe and all our gear into a trailer and towed it behind our ancient ATV. We were Daryl's guests, and since at least a half dozen orange-clad deer hunters were perched on stands throughout the woods along the trail that morning, Mike and I wisely chose to wait until around 9 a.m. to begin our duck hunt rather than go out before dawn and likely spook deer.

Our camouflaged canoe, burdened with two dozen decoys, a hefty lunch, thermos, two boxes of magnum steel shells and guns, crashed through quarter inch thick ice as we shoved it out into the lake's bay. The sheet of hard water stretched 50 yards out into the lake, where it merged into gray liquid. The sound of crinkling ice reverberated down the shoreline as the canoe knifed outward.

Forty-five minutes later, Mike and I were settled in a makeshift blind amidst a long finger of cattails. Twenty-eight decoys gently rode the waves in front of our blind as low gray clouds scampered across the sky. The air temperature was slightly below freezing, and our every exhalation was readily visible in the frosty air. The frozen silence of the bay was occasionally broken by the boom of a shotgun with slugs to the west, but more frequently by three quick shots over the lake—another missed duck, most likely.

Such poignant memories of a late season duck hunt. But foremost in my memory bank is the ducks themselves . . . man, there were ducks! At any given moment during our stay in the blind, great flocks could be seen trading back and forth across the big lake. There were big groups of huge northern mallards, evidencing a wariness borne of three months of gunning pressure on their southern journey. Those birds never did drop into our decoys. Several flocks warily circled a few times, questioning our pleading calls. But invariably they would notice something alarming, and they'd depart, climbing higher into the grey sky. On that particular day, though, most of the ducks were divers—squadrons of redheads, small groups of Cans, an occasional flock of tiny buffleheads, but huge aggregations of bluebills and ringnecks. From nowhere they seemed to come, some of them knifing through the thick sky in a downward thrust, plunging like shooting stars toward the welcome water. Others skimmed the water so low that their wings got wet, so low they totally escaped our radar. Those were the ducks I still recall today. Ducks that drop from the heavens can quickly be spotted, and a hunter can slip the safety off, jump up and touch off a quick shot or two at the birds as they strafe the outer fringe of the decoy spread . . . and then create an excuse for missing badly. But those "sneakers"—the ones that all of the sudden appear right over the dekes, just a foot off the water, still doing 60 mph and showing no signs of braking—they were the ones I remember, the ones I never managed to swing on. And now, eight months later, I still see them, hear them, experience them. Diving ducks!

Mike and I managed to collect six diving ducks that November day, all of them bluebills and ringnecks. None of them presented an easy shot, but at least they flew close enough to our decoys that we could connect. The day's highlight, though, came when a pair of big mallards drifted in from directly out in front. They momentarily set their wings, giving us hope that they would drop in. But at about 60 yards, they turned on the steam again and climbed directly over our blind. Mike and I both leaped up, and since we were shooting 3 inch shells and there was open water all around us, we decided to go for it. At our shots, both birds shuddered and lost altitude but kept flying in spite of our second shots.

The two mallards split apart, and mine rapidly dropped and finally splashed into the water 150 yards out. Mike's duck, however, a fine big drake with brilliant plumage, locked its wings and sailed across the bay, then all of the sudden collapsed and seemed to fall dead into the woods. We carefully marked the spot, then launched the canoe to retrieve my cripple. We were soon within range, and I dispatched it on the water—a heavy bodied female. We turned toward the shore, eyeing the spot where Mike's bird had gone down. We beached the canoe and split up, combing the ground in front of us, and after just three minutes, Mike hollered for me. Lying stone dead on a deer trail in the middle of the woods was the big drake. And on its leg was a USFWS band, which later notified us that the bird was 5 ½ years old and had been banded on one of the prairie potholes of Manitoba. What a trophy! The Fish and Wildlife Service annually bands thousands of ducks, but a very small percentage of those bands are recovered, since most waterfowl die from non-hunting causes. For that reason, a banded bird in a hunter's bag is a rare find.

When you are hunched in a cattail blind on a cold gray November morning and the sky above you is forever punctuated by tiny missiles knifing earthward, it makes you feel suddenly very small. Many of these waterfowl were likely hatched on the prairie marshes of Manitoba a year or two earlier. An unrelenting force drove them to abandon their summer homes in late August and wing their way toward the Gulf of Mexico thousands of miles distant. Precisely what triggered their departure? How was their flight guided? We may never completely answer these and other questions about waterfowl, and that is just fine with me. God is much bigger than I am. I will never comprehend his creation, but I do want to learn more about it. That is what keeps drawing me back to the sloughs in autumn. Sometimes I wonder if God created ducks just for guys like me. I'd like to think so. I'm thankful He did.

Psalm 104: 24, 33:

How many are your works, Oh Lord! In wisdom you made them all; the earth is full of your creatures. I will sing to the Lord all my life; I will sing praise to my God as long as I live.

A FOOT LAKE LESSON

One perfect spring day, a rare occasion when the wind was not blasting through at 25 mph, I called Sheri from school and announced we were going fishing after work. Walleye season had already been open for a week, and I hadn't been out since opening day even though word was out that the walleyes were hitting.

With the confidence and optimism born of 20 years of professional guiding experience, we trailered down to the local "hot" lake, where I had heard that everyone was taking limits of fish. There are two times of the year when walleyes can be ridiculously "easy"—spring and late fall. Never being one to overwork, I usually try to take advantage of those poor walleyes during these magic fishing windows, then I let them rest during the summer season, when I concentrate more fully on bass and northerns.

I had collected night crawlers after a recent rainfall, but just for insurance, we stopped at the local bait shop and picked up a couple dozen fathead minnows. A jig/minnow combination rarely fails in the spring, and it also happens to be the favorite technique for both Sheri and me. Jim, the bait shop proprietor, confirmed the reports I'd heard about Foot Lake; the fish were still active.

Sheri and I launched the boat and parked the truck alongside two dozen other vehicles, which led me to believe that we had indeed chosen the right lake. Fishermen may have a reputation for being extremely secretive about their "hot" holes, but when a good walleye bite is on, word gets out quickly. As we pulled up to my first spot on the lake, I began rigging Sheri's rod with a jig and minnow, and I tied on a Lindy rig and tipped it with a crawler. Experience has shown it is a good idea to begin with two separate offerings on any given day in order to discover the walleyes' preference. We quickly found out that, on this spot at least, the fish wanted neither of our offerings. Either they weren't using this area (difficult to discern, as the water was only six feet deep, thus presenting a very narrow view on the depthfinder) or they simply were refusing our offerings. I had so much confidence in our two presentations that I figured the former guess was correct, so we promptly reeled in and headed for another spot.

This scenario was repeated at every spot I picked out. We tried casting floating Rapalas, rattle baits, and shallow diving crankbaits, and we tried slow trolling Lindy Rigs and jigs. In short, I tried every option my professional mind could conjure up—still not one hit.

My optimism had long ago waned, but I still had two more "hot" spots to work. As we neared the first, I counted five other boats patrolling the area—a good sign. I quietly eased into position, and Sheri and I both began casting. I noticed that the boat closest to us was anchored. It had four occupants: a man and woman with two small kids, both of whom were busy scurrying around the boat as only kids can do. I don't know how much quality walleye fishing can be accomplished while tending to the needs and desires of two small kids who have a penchant for long casts, tangled lines, and spilled pop. But I mentally commended the couple for taking their kids out and introducing them to fishing.

I began pitching a jig and minnow in all directions because we were fishing a large "flat," an area void of structure of any kind. The couple in the other boat seemed to be having difficulty with their reels and with trying to prevent their kids from creating utter pandemonium. I gave the area fifteen minutes, slowly moving around with the electric trolling motor. Not one strike.

Discouraged, I decided to leave and try my last spot. This spot was also a "flat" of sorts, but it held deeper water nearby, and it was much larger with some scattered vegetation. I decided trolling a crankbait would be the best option because it would allow us to cover the most water in the shortest amount of time. The decision proved to be a viable one, for though it didn't exactly fill the livewell, it did provide two small "eaters" over the next 20 minutes or so. The action was certainly much slower than I had anticipated, so Sheri and I reluctantly reeled in, packed up our gear, and cranked up the 90 for the ride to the ramp.

We flew across the lake, and I throttled down as we approached the access. To my dismay, I observed a small lineup of boats outside the access, all idling in position, patiently (or in some cases, impatiently) waiting their turn. The delay was apparently due to one boat operator who was experiencing difficulty backing his car down to the water or putting his boat onto the trailer—or both. Then I recognized the boat. It belonged to the couple with the two kids. After watching the man for a full minute, it became apparent to me that the man was a neophyte at loading and unloading his boat, so I immediately decided to offer him a hand, since it seemed the Christian thing to do. And it would get me off the lake quicker.

The gentleman gladly accepted my offer of a helping hand, so I jumped onto his trailer, grabbed the rope, and aided him in swinging the boat into position so I could winch it up. It was then I noticed the four fishing rods strewn about the boat's floor. Snapped onto the end of the monofilament line on each reel was a hideously bright, fluorescent chartreuse plastic worm six inches long. I laughed inwardly, and probably smiled outwardly, at the thought of pitching that glitzy, garish creation into the water in hopes of outwitting the wily walleye.

"This is our first time fishing walleyes, actually," the gentleman said as I began winching up his boat.

"No kidding!" I thought, but said nothing.

"In fact we've only had our boat in the water once before this. I'm not very good at loading or unloading this thing, yet. But my neighbor said the walleyes were going nuts out here, so we thought we would give it a try."

"No problem," I answered. "Glad to help you out." I couldn't rid my mind of the image of those ludicrous, brightly-colored caterpillar creations on the end of the fishing line, and I mentally calculated that this particular family was not much threat to the Foot Lake walleye population. Just as my private "smugness" about my relative fishing know-how was about to erase the recent memory of today's poor catch, I heard a familiar flapping noise from inside the man's boat. First one walleye, then another, then a couple more, and finally an entire two person limit on a yellow rope stringer slid out from underneath the middle seat. And they were *nice* ones, certainly a lot larger than my two "cigars."

I couldn't believe it! A husband and wife team with virtually no walleye experience and a seemingly total lack of common sense regarding terminal tackle had just totally blown me out of the water. To this day, I've never again heard of a walleye limit taken on bright neon yellow plastic worms! My afternoon, which had begun with confidence, perhaps even cockiness, ended in utter frustration. I honestly don't mind slow fishing . . . when everyone else is experiencing the same lack of success. But in my profession, I am paid to be able to unlock the "secrets"—the secret lures, secret spots, secret techniques.

That was not the first time, nor the last, that my heavenly Father shrouded my world with a heavy (and healthy) dose of humility. Most of us need it fairly regularly, yet we would never ask for it. I suppose that is why God doles it out when we least wish for it.

Luke 14:7–11:

When he noticed how the guests picked the places of honor at the table, he told them this parable: "When someone invites you to a wedding feast, do not take the place of honor, for a person more distinguished than you may have been invited. If so, the host who invited both of you will come and say to you, "Give this man your seat."

Then, humiliated, you will have to take the least important place. But when you are invited, take the lowest place, so that when your host comes, he will say to you, "Friend, move up to a better place." Then you will be honored in the presence of all your fellow guests. For everyone who exalts himself will be humbled, and he who humbles himself will be exalted.

THE FLU BUCK

Deer hunting around my west central Minnesota home hardly qualifies as legitimate deer hunting. Unobstructed, flat farm country necessitates the use of a shotgun with slugs rather than a high-power rifle. That alone may relegate the hunt to a second class status. Additionally, a hunter may only choose one of two options—a weekend hunt on the first week of the season, or a four day hunt during the second week. For me, this translates to a Saturday/Sunday hunt, or more typically a Saturday hunt, since Sunday is set aside as a day of traditional worship.

With just one day out of 365 in which to bag a legal deer, the day tends to become a rather "big event." Maybe not as monumental as during those bygone years in northern Minnesota when schools were closed because teachers did not want to teach to empty classrooms, but "big" nonetheless. It is a day soaked with memories of past hunts, nervous anticipation of a trophy buck, and endless ritualistic preparations. This said, you might relate to my complete disappointment when my son Mike came down with a severe case of stomach flu the day before deer season in 1996. Mike and his wife, Heather, live in the Twin Cities area two hours away. On Friday afternoon, as I was making final preparations for the next day's hunt, the phone rang. It was Heather.

"Mike is sick with the flu; he's thrown up twice since he got home from work."

My heart sank, but I advised him to go to bed for a couple hours, then try to make the trip, anyway. Perhaps this was only a 12 hour bug and Mike would be fine by morning. Mike acquiesced, and shortly after midnight, after five unscheduled stops on the road's shoulder, they pulled into our driveway. We immediately tucked Mike into bed, hoping and praying that in five hours he would be recovered.

At 5 a.m., I rolled Mike out of bed, but by the peaked look on his face, I knew these particular prayers had not been answered. Mike persevered for the first two hours of the hunt. Normally he was the one we called on to do the bulk of the work on our hunt; it was Mike who was always chosen to push through the densest cattails; it was Mike who would sprint around to the end of a piece of cover so we could drive it; and it was Mike who always dragged out my big buck—or at least if I ever shoot one, he will eagerly drag it out. But today, his normally fit and strong body was letting him down, and though most of his nausea was gone, his body was still suffering the ravages of a relentless case of the flu.

Reluctantly, Mike agreed I should drop him off at the house to rest for a couple hours. The remaining five men in our party hunted hard the rest of the day, and we managed to bag three deer in the process. At 3 o'clock, we drove back to the house and found Mike awake, up and dressed. The nap had done wonders, and though he didn't feel fully recovered, he informed us he was ready to hunt the final two hours. The day he had been anticipating for almost a year was practically finished, and he hadn't been able to participate. What a bummer! I was thinking how fitting it would be if Mike could connect during our final drive. Unfortunately, we saw no more deer, so as the sun set, Mike said farewell to a deer season that wasn't.

That night, just before Mike turned in for the night, he suggested we sit on stand the next morning at sunrise. Quickly my mind contemplated the logistics of this plan; I had to teach Sunday school at 9 a.m., so it would make for a very rushed morning. But this would be our last chance to hunt deer together this season, so I set the alarm for 5 a.m.

A cool and cloudy but calm day greeted us as we walked in darkness toward our predetermined spot Sunday morning. With time at a premium, our choices were limited, so we had opted for a public area just 3 miles from the house. It held a large grove and shelterbelt in addition to a 100 acre slough. The chances of Mike getting a deer were minimal because the area had been hunted hard the day before, but the choice was better than sleeping in on the final morning of the deer season. Mike perched himself on a bucket next to a well-worn deer trail on the northwest side of the grove, and I skirted around to the southern extremity, where I sat on a little knoll overlooking both the grove and the slough. Mike and I were separated by 200 yards, though we couldn't see each other through the dense brush.

As expected, the time passed too quickly and too uneventfully. Except for the early rising songbirds, the occasional cackle of a rooster pheasant, and one cottontail rabbit, I heard and saw nothing while on stand. Finally it was time for me to head home and prepare for Sunday school; Mike could stay an additional hour before it was time for church. I rose, picked up my bucket, took a long look all around me, and started back toward the truck.

Suddenly, as if a vapor, it appeared in front of me, at the fringe of the grove—a plump deer standing broadside, staring directly at me, scarcely 50 yards away. I slid the bucket to the ground, clicked off the safety and raised my gun. I could hardly believe it as I put the bead on her shoulder. Then a strange sensation came over me; I didn't need this deer. If anyone needed a shot this morning, it was Mike. This was supposed to be *his* deer. But the chances of Mike seeing this deer were slim to none. The situation was so bizarre and improbable. Why wasn't this deer bolting away at full speed? It had obviously spotted me. And then, to compound my amazement, the deer stepped forward, and I saw antlers. It was a nice young buck! Still, it just stood there, looking at me. I put the gun up again; never in my life had I passed up a legal buck. But instead of squeezing the trigger, I slowly lowered my shotgun. Somehow, some way, I had to turn this buck toward Mike. Slowly, I stepped forward into plain view of the deer. It took a couple steps away, and I followed. I started skirting around the deer, then walked closer, all the while my heart racing. After I had closed the gap by ten yards or so, the buck decided this was enough, and he started trotting away. I broke into a dead run toward him, and then he bolted through the grove and toward the thick shelterbelt. At the top of my lungs I shouted,

"Coming toward you, Mike!"

On the other side of the grove, Mike heard my cry but didn't understand what I said. All he heard were some unintelligible words, then "Mike!" His first instinct was that I needed help, so he jumped up off his bucket and began sprinting toward me. All of the sudden he stopped, wondering if just maybe I had spooked a deer toward him. He turned to head back to his stand, when a fat six-point buck burst through the brush and practically collided with him. By then I was running toward where Mike should be, and I heard his shotgun boom—once.

I hit the deer trail and sprinted along it toward Mike's stand and found him standing over the dead buck, a mile-wide grin on his face.

"Thanks, Dad! He ran right at me!"

I've been hunting deer for over 20 years. In all that time, I've never seen a "dumb" or uneducated buck during the season. This one was a pure anomaly. He saw me, yet did not spook. He showed no fear in spite of eluding hunters the day before. He ran in precisely the only direction which would present Mike with a shot. And he ran right up to Mike. Absolutely the only rationale I can come up with is that I wasn't the only one feeling sorry for Mike the day before. Just maybe God decided that Mike really needed this buck. Mike hadn't complained or grumbled once about his misfortune the day before; he accepted it as "one of those things." But God definitely paid him back on this Sunday morning. I wasn't even late for Sunday school. And Mike was only ten minutes late for church.

Ephesians 6:18:

And pray in the Spirit on all occasions with all kinds of prayers and requests. With this in mind, be alert and always keep on praying for all the saints.

THE FISHING OPENER

Each year, sometime in late December, I stop in at our local bank to pick up one of those handy, pocket-sized appointment calendars. It is my attempt to finally become organized. In this booklet all my summer guiding trips are recorded, but in addition, you will find many other important dates, such as teacher workshops, the exam schedule, vacation dates, the odd wedding . . . plus a variety of "opening days," such as ducks, pheasants, grouse, deer, bass, and walleye. Of these, only two are of paramount significance, the duck opener and the walleye opener. I probably would not even need to record those two, because as soon as they are announced to the public, the dates become fixed in my mind.

Indeed, the Minnesota walleye opener is pretty heady stuff. Friday afternoon before the midnight opener, all major highways heading north are clogged, and two out of every three vehicles will be towing boats. Enterprising young kids sit on strategic intersections selling freshly dug nightcrawlers. All the hype is likely not totally warranted, as mid-May weather often precludes any truly great fishing.

I can remember pulling into the town of Walker one opener at about 6 a.m., when the bank thermometer announced 28 degrees and my windshield wipers were on high speed in a vain attempt to provide clear vision through the horizontal sleet. On such an occasion, there's not a snowmobile suit made that can make a day on the water comfortable. On the other hand, I have also returned in the afternoon thoroughly sunburned after an eight hour stint under clear blue skies on a Minnesota walleye opener.

Just four years ago, the Minnesota walleye opener brought more typical weather than either of those two extremes. The weatherman promised a day of 65 degrees with ample sunshine and a light breeze out of the west. Rarely is a walleye opener met with such ideal conditions, so it was with much optimism that I greeted the shores of Lake Winnibigoshish that Saturday morning. My two fishing partners were sons Mike and Mark—a very unusual treat these days, as the boys are grown and leading their own busy lives, often far from home. But both boys happened to be home for the weekend, so the gigantic red sun that inched above the treetops witnessed the three of us sliding my 16' Sylvan into the chilly waters of Cutfoot Sioux on the northeast shore of the big lake.

Winnibigoshish: this classic walleye lake, where opening day is as traditional for some anglers as Christmas or New Years Day is to most of us, and every bit as festive, lies just fifty miles north of our cabin. Its 70,000 acres and 116 miles of shoreline rank it fourth in size among Minnesota lakes, behind Red, Mille Lacs, and Leech. This body of water is technically a reservoir rather than a natural lake, for its boundaries were artificially created when the Mississippi River's flow was impeded by a set of dams. Its charm lies, however, not so much in its origins as in its personality and its potential. Nestled among the towering Norway pines of the Chippewa National Forest, this windswept, round basin is officially called Lake Winnibigoshish, literally translated "Big Windy Water" in Ojibway. As mentioned in an earlier chapter, most fishermen who spend any amount of time bouncing on her waves affectionately call her Big Winnie.

After launching the boat, I drove the truck almost a quarter mile along the dusty gravel road leading into Cutfoot Sioux before I found a parking spot. Seeing all the pickups and SUV's with trailers, I knew what awaited us out on Winnie—armadas with scores, perhaps even hundreds of boats in concert, drifting or trolling the shallow north shores. By mid-May, the sand and gravel shoreline had been buffeted for two weeks with the prevailing southerly wind; those same shorelines would draw the anglers because most of the walleyes in the entire lake would be attracted to these ideal spawning areas.

I warmed up the 90 horsepower Johnson as we slowly motored out from shore, bundling up for the chilly one-mile ride out to the "Flats," the first choice for 90% of the anglers here today. I fastened my parka hood firmly, punched the throttle, and the boat leaped up on plane; we were off! Ten minutes later, faces bright red and tear streaked, we approached Bowens Flats, where 300 or more boats were greeting the new walleye season.

I skirted around the entire group to reach the southern edge of the armada, then killed the motor to begin our slow drift to the north. I can remember standing up behind the console and walking to the bow of the boat. I had a chartreuse Northland Lipstick jig tied onto my line, and I dressed it with a lively shiner minnow. With my right arm, I quickly flipped the jig overboard into eight feet of water, clicked the bail shut, then reached down with my left arm to swing my electric motor into position. I never finished the motion. As I bent down, my line went taut, and my rod tip dipped and danced ever so slightly. I set the hook. A walleye already! Five seconds into the trip, even before I had lowered the electric motor to begin our drift, I was battling a good fish!

I will not attempt to describe how good that felt. When fishing is a lifestyle rather than a hobby, and you haven't had a fishing rod in your hands for five months, then even a two pound walleye on the other end of a lightweight graphite rod is pure ecstasy.

Unbelievably, the entire morning was just about that fast. By noon our minnow buckets were empty; we had used all the shiners, then all the fatheads, and even the few floating dead ones. Toward the end, out of curiosity and desperation, Mark slipped on a chartreuse Shad Rap, and in fifteen minutes of casting off the stern of the boat, caught five more fat male walleyes. By 1 o'clock, we were tired, content, and satisfied, and with a couple meals of fresh walleyes swimming in the livewell, we headed back toward the landing. My log book shows we boated 45 walleyes that morning, plus dozens of perch and a few northerns.

That trip was special. There was lots of laughter, joking, and kidding as usual, plus lots of hook-setting. But it wasn't the fishing that made the day so memorable. Nor the weather. Not even the company. Rather, the circumstances. You see, I was fishing with Mike and Mark. And on their list of things they like to do, walleye fishing ranks pretty low. Mention ducks, and they stop breathing. Ask if they would like to do some pheasant or grouse hunting, and they'll drop everything. But when it comes to fishing, well, it had better be for bass. To leave a warm bed at 4 a.m. with the prospect of facing a raw wind in search of the often lethargic walleye is more of a sacrifice. But the boys knew that I like walleyes, especially on opening day. I suspect they just wanted to spend the day with the old man doing what he liked to do.

That is a mark of maturity. To put others before self is to mirror what Christ always did for us. Of all the themes preached in the Gospels, servanthood seems to be one of the most prominent. My boys probably hardly remember the trip; I will never forget it.

Ephesians 5:1–7:

Be imitators of God, therefore, as dearly loved children and live a life of love, just as Christ loved us and gave himself up for us as a fragrant offering and sacrifice to God. But among you there must not be even a hint of sexual immorality, or of any kind of impurity, or of greed, because these are improper for God's holy people. Nor should there be obscenity, foolish talk or coarse joking, which are out of place, but rather thanksgiving. For of this you can be sure: No immoral, impure or greedy person—such a man is an idolater—has any inheritance in the kingdom of Christ and of God. Let no one deceive you with empty words, for because of such things God's wrath comes on those who are disobedient. Therefore do not be partners with them.

BIRDS OF A COLOR

I was on the access road to Island Lake one fresh spring morning when the trees were sprouting their brand new lime-green clusters of leaves. White-barked birches offered up their green gifts toward a cloudless blue sky. Suddenly, against this sea of green flitted a brilliant splash of red as a male scarlet tanager lit on a pendulous bough alongside the road. I braked, allowing my clients to view the stunning songbird, which was as conspicuous as a blaze-orange stocking cap in a duck blind. The tanager evidenced no fear of our intrusion; in fact, it allowed us ample time to appreciate his spring splendor. A photo of the bird still adorns the wall behind my desk, and I am forever struck with the vivid contrast between the scarlet feathers and the chartreuse leaves.

Have you ever wondered *why* God created what He did? In other words, way back in the beginning when God created all the major life forms (I realize God is still busy creating today, as new species are constantly being fashioned; biologists have named but a fraction of the organisms on Earth), why did he not create just one kind of bird?

You know, with predictable regularity, snow falls on a substantial portion of the Earth, but to my knowledge it always falls white. God created snow to be but one color, yet no matter how often we experience it, we are always struck by its sparkling "whiteness." Why not just one color of bird? God could have built a generic bird, one with the capability to adjust to every available niche, and one that is drab brown. We could just as well be surrounded with millions of starlings or house sparrows or grackles. Had we never known otherwise, such an avian creation would not appear strange, but normal. I believe I would think no less of God's creative capability even if He had made all birds alike.

Instead, God made it part of His plan to enrich our lives to a degree none of us fully fathoms—and daily we have the privilege of seeing splashes of red in the overhead branches, streaks of indigo darting through the sky, and bright yellows flitting among the underbrush. Even in my wintery backyard in the desolate plains of west central Minnesota, visitors to my feeders will include black-capped chickadees, white and red breasted nut-hatches, downy and hairy and red-bellied woodpeckers, blue jays, juncos, and house sparrows. What a dull world this would be if we did not notice all this variety unfolding around us! But do we?

We fill our lives with so many trivialities that we leave no time for the truly significant—such as seeing God's handiwork immediately around us.

Recently, I walked down to Wubben's Slough, a sprawling public hunt-ing area three miles down the road from our house. The late April morning was full of its spring braggadocio as I perched myself atop a small bluff overlooking the water. Migrating waterfowl dotted the entire slough, and the morning sun bestowed all the drakes with an iridescent brilliance borne only from newly formed breeding plumages. From the diminutive green-wing teal to the gigantic Canada goose, the entertainment was nothing short of spectacular. In the brief span of one-half hour, I identified fifteen species of waterfowl cavorting and courting in the fertile slough water. What incredible diversity!

At home, many chores awaited me; there were papers to grade, lessons to be formulated, even lawn work to be done. Time was slipping away, yet here I was, quietly sitting, watching, listening, doing nothing. But I decided that at that moment in time, nothing was more important or more worthy of my time than this—praising God again for creating ducks and geese to migrate, not only through central Minnesota in April, but through my life as well.

If we assume that each "little brown bird" flitting among the bushes is a house sparrow, we make a monumental mistake. Picking up a pair of binocu-lars could reveal a dash of yellow on the crown or a snow-white patch under the throat, or even freckles of red streaking the breast, and it would open a whole new world of discovery, yielding just a small glimpse of God's immea-surable creative diversity. May we begin to notice more . . . then observe more . . . then appreciate more the diversity around us. May that in turn lead us to praise God even more.

Psalm 8:

O Lord, our Lord, how majestic is your name in all the earth! You have set your glory above the heavens. From the lips of children and infants you have ordained praise because of your enemies, to silence the foe and the avenger.

When I consider your heavens, the work of your fingers, the moon and the stars, which you have set in place, what is man that you are mindful of him, the son of man that you care for him? You made him a little lower than the heavenly beings and crowned him with glory and honor. You made him ruler over the works of your hands; you put everything under his feet, all flocks and herds, and the beasts of the field, the birds of the air, and the fish of the sea, all that swim the paths of the seas.

O Lord, our Lord, how majestic is your name in all the earth!

BE STILL AND KNOW THAT I AM GOD

I don't know how else to describe them besides "war whoops." Of course, I've never heard an actual war whoop, but these are loud, sudden punctuation marks, and they're reserved for ultra special occasions. I've been party to them occasionally in my sporting pursuits.

There was our deer hunt five years ago, when Mike and I and the four Zimmer boys were pushing a large patch of heavy cattails during mid-day. Our experience has been that as deer get driven on opening day, they often seek refuge in the heaviest cover to be found. We had posted two guys on the far end of this slough, and four of us were slugging our way through the cattails, creating plenty of commotion to rouse any whitetails.

Sheer luck was with us, for Mike walked right up onto a beautiful, wide-racked eight-point buck, and the monster erupted almost from under his feet, charging straight away in a mighty burst of speed. It presented a pure, instinctive "pheasant" shot, and Mike threw up his Browning A-5 and touched the trigger. At 20 yards, the slug found the buck's neck, and the great animal tumbled head-over-heels. Even through the heavy cover, I could see tumbling antlers and hooves. And, over on the next mile road, another party of hunters heard Mike's "whoop!" In several years of deer hunting together, our party had shot its share of bucks, but until now we'd never taken a trophy. This head was worthy of the wall.

There was also the time in Ontario when six of us guys in two boats were on an early morning northern pike run before breakfast. From our boat, I watched as my son-in-law, Chad, cast a silver and blue Rat-L-Trap over a bed of healthy green "cabbage" weeds, then mightily set the hook on a big fish. We slowly motored closer as the action progressed, watching Chad play the fish around the front of the boat. After three mighty runs, Ron Bouma thrust the landing net under 41 inches of very healthy, fat northern pike. The heavy fish barely fit into the net as Ron quickly lifted it up and into the boat. Chad's "whoop!" was probably noted back in camp four miles to the west.

These spontaneous, explosive outbursts are about as unnatural and as out of place as the report of a shotgun itself. In stark contrast, picture with me if you will, a quiet sunrise in any marsh in mid-duck season, when all the local ducks have already departed and the northern birds have not yet arrived. A session in a blind in such circumstances can be a lesson in futility, disappointment, and failure; that is, if your primary goal is to kill a duck. But what a joy, what a sublime experience it can be to reflect, meditate, and converse with God.

Recently, both my sons and I had the privilege of sharing a duck blind in just such circumstances, except we were entertaining a sunset rather than a sunrise. The day was an unusual one for late October, with temperatures in the mid 60s and scarcely a hint of a breeze under blue skies. Two dozen mallard decoys sat placidly in the murky slough water before us, their perfect reflections casting a surreal atmosphere to the afternoon. Not once during the entire evening did the honk of a goose or quack of a duck break the peaceful silence of the slough. I studied a disintegrating jet trail while mesmerized by a bank of unique pink clouds before the sun. As evening progressed, waves of red-winged blackbirds drifted into the cattails for their nightly roost. Flocks of unidentifiable shorebirds spun and dove in unison just above the water in front of me. Occasionally a flock of gulls on the distant horizon momentarily fooled me into thinking they were ducks, but they invariably turned out to be . . . well, just gulls.

Methodically, I scanned the entire slough before me, from left horizon to right horizon, periodically swiveling on my stool to peer behind me as well. Experience has taught me that it is always the unsuspecting, inquisitive teal that flies straight into the decoys from out front, but the prized mallard tends to sneak in from behind, managing to escape totally unscathed. I was not about to let that happen this time.

In spite of my watchful eye, however, the slough was barren on this day. Everything I saw and smelled reminded me I was duck hunting. Two wooden calls draped from my neck, clunking against each other each time I swiveled. The once rich bluing on the receiver of my ancient Browning autoloader was long-since worn away, but the unmistakable aroma of Hoppe's #9 occasionally wafted up to my nostrils. Neoprene waders allowed me to sit in comfort in my camouflaged canoe, but the muck and mud caked on their boots reminded me I was still in a slough.

After an hour of searching with hopeful eyes, the total serenity and peace of my surroundings enveloped me. I sat there, hunched down on my stool and began praying. My "official" prayer list was at home, tucked inside my Bible where I consulted it each morning. Even without the list, though, the names of a dozen friends, acquaintances, and even a couple people I hardly knew came to mind—a 33-year-old former student with bone cancer; an energetic, newly married 23-year-old gal with Hodgkins; a dear friend with Parkinsons; and a couple whose 17-year-old daughter was heavily into alcohol, marijuana, and likely, sex. The list of traumas and sad scenarios could go on and on—so many people whose fortunes were nowhere near so blessed as mine at that moment. Now was the perfect time to lay the needs of those people before the Lord.

I then concluded with a time of praise. It could not be helped. It was impossible to sit there and not be reminded that God is *the* God of the entire universe and worthy of my praise. There could be nothing so still, so serene, so worshipful as this slough right now. My preference perhaps would be to have the evening sky ripped by a flock of canvasbacks descending into my decoys, but that was not to be. The complete lack of ducks—in fact the total lack of activity—became loud in its silence. I have found that I can worship God through many diverse activities. He often speaks to me in his loudest, clearest voice, however, when I am utterly silent.

Ecclesiastes 5:1–3, 7:

Guard your steps when you go to the house of God. Go near to listen rather than to offer the sacrifice of fools, who do not know that they do wrong. Do not be quick with your mouth, do not be hasty in your heart to utter anything before God. God is in heaven and you are on earth, so let your words be few. As a dream comes when there are many cares, so the speech of a fool when there are many words. Much dreaming and many words are meaningless. Therefore stand in awe of God.

GOD IS GOOD

One hundred years ago, a Canada goose sighting anywhere in the United States was such a rare occasion that when the postmaster of the tiny Eastern town of St. Michaels shot one, it was hung from the post office door so the townsfolk could marvel at the unusual bird. Even in my early waterfowling days thirty years ago, Canada geese were a "no-show" over the marshes of Minnesota.

It is with more than a little wonder then that we reflect upon the current status of the Canada goose. It seems ironic that as the passion for waterfowling has progressed unabated over the decades, the population of Canada geese has also risen to unprecedented levels.

In fact, one particular sub-species, the giant Canada goose, has become so numerous around my west-central Minnesota home that the US Fish & Wildlife Service has entertained a variety of bizarre measures in an attempt to stem their ever-increasing numbers. Local farmers lodge the majority of the complaints, and rightfully so, as I'm told an adult giant Canada can consume ten pounds of corn per day in preparation for migration. And in the spring, after the goslings have hatched, the adults often lead their troops of young ones straight down the rows of newly emerging corn plants, where each stem is unceremoniously plucked from the fertile ground by the invading young geese. Last year, the ambitious pilfering of crops led the USFWS to issue permits to many local farmers, enabling them to destroy baby geese on their farmland. A farmer's profit margin simply does not allow for philanthropic feelings toward geese.

In addition to such unique methods of goose control, the USFWS has also engaged in more traditional practices, such as extending hunting seasons and liberalizing bag limits. This past season, we were again granted an early goose season, opening almost a month prior to the general waterfowl hunting season. And so it was that opening day 2000 found Mike and Mark and me heading out to our favorite slough before sunrise.

In the mosquito-infested pre-dawn, the boys and I made our way toward the cattails lining the slough, where we hoped to intercept the geese on their morning flight from the slough to their current feeding plot, a wheat field just one half mile to the north. We agreed it would be more enjoyable for the three of us to sit together, but more productive if we split up and spread out along the slough's edge. That way we could maximize the chances of one of us getting a shot. So as the sun eased its way above the eastern horizon, the boys and I were each separated by about 100 yards. From here on, it was a guessing game. There were geese on the water, as we could hear by their periodic honking, and we knew they would soon lift off to feed. The question was whether they would fly our way. And if so, which of us would get shooting, if any?

Ten minutes after sunrise, there was a loud clamor as geese rose off the water. My heart pounded in nervous anticipation, then it quickly sank when the honking faded in the distance as a dozen geese flew out the opposite side of the slough. Within minutes, the slough grew quiet again but for the occasional cluck of a feeding coot or the raspy quack of a fly-by mallard hen. As I huddled in the damp slough grass, basking deeply in every smell and sound of this—my first hunt of the year—and reveling in my good fortune at being here with my two boys, an incredibly loud commotion arose from the slough as a huge flock of Canadas unanimously lifted off. I pitched forward into the cattails to fully conceal myself, then waited, not having a clue which direction the great birds were heading. It seemed as though the noise was growing louder, so I chanced a peek through the vegetation; they were coming! Only then did I comprehend the size of this flock. It was huge! And the birds were barely skimming the water; they would have to climb in order to avoid the cattails rimming the slough.

Instantly, the geese were on top of me, and I slid the safety off my Browning Over/Under, swung on the nearest honking black and white object, and touched the trigger . . . and missed. In my excitement, I swung too far ahead of the low-flying birds. Quickly correcting, I swung on the same bird again and crumpled it with my second shot. Oblivious to all else around me, I dashed out into the waist-high slough grass where my bird went down. As I ran through the weeds I glanced to my left and noticed that Mark too was sprinting. He must have dropped one, also! Immediately, I looked right and saw Mike emerging from the cattails with one big Canada in his grip. What an incredible ten seconds we had just experienced! One large flock of geese had spread out and drifted over all three of us, giving each of us a good shot, and we had responded with three clean kills.

God had devised an unlikely script, and it played out more beautifully than if we had attempted to write it ourselves. The new season had been ushered in with a literal bang, and the three of us will never forget that day when three geese dropped out of the September sky before three simultaneous guns. We bowed in thanks for our good fortune and realized once again that God is *always* good—something our frail minds often fail to comprehend, and something our sinful minds often fail to acknowledge.

Psalm 103:1–5:

Praise the Lord, O my soul; all my inmost being, praise his holy name. Praise the Lord, O my soul, and forget not all his benefits—who forgives all your sins and heals all your diseases, who redeems your life from the pit and crowns you with love and compassion, who satisfies your desires with good things so that your youth is renewed like the eagle's.

MONSTER PIKE

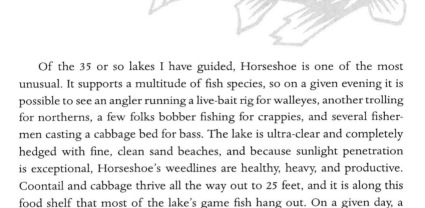

Of the 35 or so lakes I have guided, Horseshoe is one of the most unusual. It supports a multitude of fish species, so on a given evening it is possible to see an angler running a live-bait rig for walleyes, another trolling for northerns, a few folks bobber fishing for crappies, and several fishermen casting a cabbage bed for bass. The lake is ultra-clear and completely hedged with fine, clean sand beaches, and because sunlight penetration is exceptional, Horseshoe's weedlines are healthy, heavy, and productive. Coontail and cabbage thrive all the way out to 25 feet, and it is along this food shelf that most of the lake's game fish hang out. On a given day, a couple good fishermen can ply the miles of weedline with spinnerbaits, crankbaits, and soft plastics and boat between 50 and 100 fish.

Now, to anyone familiar with north central Minnesota's natural lakes, this may not seem so out of the ordinary; several of my lakes are capable of 100-fish days. But Horseshoe is located right in the middle of tourist territory, where BMWs, Mercedes, and Lexuses soon threaten to rival the Chevy and Ford trucks in number. With today's frenetic rush to own a "place on a lake," it is no surprise that every last foot of Horseshoe's shoreline is fully developed and that every 100 feet or so, another dock juts out into the clear water. The lake has become crowded, not so much with visiting anglers who launch at the public access, but with all the property owners, most of whom own multiple boats, from jet skis to pontoon boats, from speedboats to bass boats. This lake is a virtual playground, especially on weekends. In spite of all the commotion, though, it holds fish . . . lots of them.

The knock on Horseshoe, if there is one, is that the fish tend to run on the small side. But if it's action a person seeks, this is the place to be, offering shallow dock fishing as well as deeper casting or trolling. And in spite of the abundance of smaller fish, this is the lake that has produced more of my true trophy bass than almost any other lake. And occasionally, the northerns run, well, monstrous.

This was dramatically illustrated one cloudy afternoon in July. I was guiding a father and son, and we were fishing the myriad of docks jutting out from north and east shores. Bright cloudless skies over Horseshoe often draw the bass to the shade, shelter, and food source of the docks. As I said, the residents of Horseshoe love their toys, and it is a very rare dock that has only one boat tied to it. Hundreds of boat lifts and canopies provide ideal habitat for bluegills and rock bass, which in turn attract the largemouths.

It only took me a couple trips onto Horseshoe to discover that all docks are not created equal. A few of them never seem to hold a bass, no matter how promising they look, while other docks function as bass magnets, virtually always producing action.

One particular dock, where a Lund Rebel and a big Crestliner runabout are moored, produced six good bass in eight casts one morning.

Well, on this particular day, the three of us were using spinning gear to throw 7" Berkley Power Worms rigged Texas style toward any shaded pockets around the docks. We were having a ball, and though the fish were a little on the young side, we were hooking lots of them, and there were enough three-pounders sandwiched in among them to keep us optimistic. Soon, however, a broad band of clouds drifted in from the western horizon, and what began as a bright sunny day slipped into a totally overcast one. Normally, I salivate with such conditions, since clouds often trigger fish much more readily than the sun. On Horseshoe, however, it can call for a complete change in tactics. The dock fish become much more difficult to take; I actually think many of them vacate the area and head to the weeds since they no longer need the shade.

Consequently, I moved out to a south weedline where thick vegetation gradually tapered into the depths rather than dropping abruptly as it does on the east shore. A western breeze allowed us to patiently drift parallel to the weed-edge while casting onto the weed tops. I began throwing a Rat-L-Trap, while the father continued with his plastic worm and the son tied on a white spinnerbait. We immediately began picking up several pint-sized bass and a few small northerns—"hammerhandles." Both bass and northerns seemed to be going on a feeding binge with the weather change, and in spite of small size, they hit and fought with an attitude.

I pitched a shad-colored bait far up onto the weed bed and began ripping it back with an erratic motion, when I got hit. Instantly, I hit back, and the solid resistance sent a shock wave up both shoulders; I was onto something very heavy! Slowly and nonchalantly, the fish swam away from the boat. I did nothing but hang on, keeping the rod tip high in the air while the drag on my baitcasting reel slowly strained. Since I had fresh 14 pound line spooled onto my reel, I wasn't worried about breaking off, but this fish was not showing any signs of slowing down. It began moving to the other side of the boat, so I followed with my rod tip, all the while keeping steady pressure. I yelled at the father to duck his head as I swung my rod over him to fight the fish off the stern of the boat. The heavy fish showed no sign of giving in, and my line steadily played out.

After about 20 seconds, the giant fish turned and headed back toward the boat. Frantically, I reeled to maintain pressure, but the fish kept coming. Then suddenly I saw it—a gigantic, dark northern cruising just under the water's surface, still headed straight toward the boat. I had never seen a northern so long, and I remember beginning to tremble.

All of the sudden, my bowed graphite baitcasting rod whipped back to its natural shape, and my heart sank as I reeled in a practically lifeless 13 inch bass, my lure firmly embedded in its jaw. Only when I noticed the two parallel gashes, roughly six inches apart and raked along the fish's side, did I realize what had happened. Apparently, the bass had slammed my lure as I retrieved it over the tops of the weeds, but then almost at the same time a huge northern had grabbed the bass sideways in its jaws, refusing to let go of an easy meal. For almost a minute, the large northern had towed the bass around, steadily taking drag. Judging by the distance between the teeth marks on the bass, and the glimpse I had of the huge northern, this was the biggest northern I've ever seen personally. I've caught pike weighing in the upper teens and also a couple legitimate fish in the 20 pound class; I believe this fish was bigger. By far.

Strangely, I felt very little dismay over losing such a huge fish. Over the years, I've lost my share of big ones. I've lost trophy bass that catapulted out of the water and spit my lure; I've had frayed line betray me as a huge northern darted under my boat. And I've even lost a big northern due to improper netting procedures. In each case, I've been devastated because each time, I realized I had screwed up. I had neglected my equipment or I had made a mental mistake in fighting the fish. Whenever that happens, I tend to beat myself up for hours after the incident. I may as well quit fishing and go home for the day because the trip is, for me, ruined. This time was different.

Absolutely nothing I had done had contributed to my losing this fish. In fact, the northern had never been hooked; she had just been tagging along for the ride. Even if she had made it to the net and I had captured it, the victory would have been bittersweet. It wouldn't have "counted" as if I'd actually outwitted the fish into striking my lure; it was not much different than snagging it.

But once again, Horseshoe had done it for me—it had put scores of fish into the boat, had given hours of pleasure to both the dad and son, and once more it had revealed a monster. That alone would draw me back to the lake another time.

Psalm 16: 5–11:

Lord, you have assigned me my portion and my cup; you have made my lot secure. The boundary lines have fallen for me in pleasant places; surely I have a delightful inheritance.

I will praise the Lord, who counsels me; even at night my heart instructs me. I have set the Lord always before me. Because he is at my right hand, I will not be shaken.

Therefore my heart is glad and my tongue rejoices; my body also will rest securely, because you will not abandon me to the grave, nor will you let your Holy One see decay.

You have made known to me the path of life; you will fill me with joy in your presence, with eternal pleasures at your right hand

THE "PRINCIPAL" OF THE THING

In the fall of 1978, our family made the transition from Iowa to Minnesota, where I assumed the responsibility of a new teaching position at Central Minnesota Christian High School in west central Minnesota. Fall is not the optimum season for a move because it happens to be my favorite time of year. Hunting and fishing are two of my passions, and September, October, and November fly by all too quickly, brim-full of waterfowl, grouse, pheasants, and walleyes.

When October rolled around in '78, it presented two problems for me. First, being a teacher meant that, for the most part, my days would be spent cooped up within four walls. The October air, blue sky, and changing leaves beckoned fiercely, but they were temptations I knew I could do nothing about. My disposition was certainly not enhanced when a couple of my buddies began making a practice of tormenting me every now and then by showing up outside my classroom window when I was in the middle of a biology lesson. They would "happen" to wander by and nonchalantly hold up a brace of Canada geese they'd just bagged or a handful of mallards and woodies. Their working hours were more flexible than mine, and that afforded them the luxury of "rubbing it in" to me periodically. Such an intrusion into my daily lesson plans would invariably ruin the rest of my day. Somehow, monocot and dicot stems just didn't hold the same charm anymore.

But an even greater dilemma soon surfaced. Since ducks are my passion, I try to spend October out in the sloughs because, by early November, much of the water is frozen and the ducks have long since departed for warmer climes. The problem is that the U.S. Fish and Wildlife Service and the Minnesota Department of Natural Resources have agreed that for the first couple weeks of the duck season, shooting hours will cease at 4 p.m. each day. The justification is that local ducks, especially mallards, benefit from those resting hours, and if they are not shot at around sunset, they may linger in an area before migrating south. But for a teacher like me, such a regulation is sheer torture.

The CMCS Teacher Handbook requires teachers to be in school each day from 8 a.m. until 3:45 p.m. Students are dismissed at 3:15, but I'm guessing it would be poor public relations if teachers trampled students at the doorway in their haste to exit school at the end of a working day—especially if their rationale is to beat the students out to the slough.

My favorite slough is only six miles from school, and personal experience has shown me that if I have my hunting gear in the truck, and I leave school promptly at 3:45, I can actually reach the cattails with about five minutes of time to shoot. Of course, I'm in no condition to actually shoot, even if a duck were to erupt right in front of me; *you* try sprinting 300 yards through tall grass in a heavy set of waders while carrying a loaded gun!

Somehow, I had to concoct a solution to this problem. The principal, Mr. Al Koning, seemed like a reasonable enough guy. He was a very stocky man with a deep, booming voice that made him somewhat intimidating. But I didn't know him well, and who knows, maybe he was approachable.

I figured I had three options in this matter. One, I could just give in and accept the notion that my duck hunting would occur on weekends only. I immediately discarded this notion in favor of something less insane. Option two was that I could try sneaking out to the parking lot early and drive off without being noticed. I debated this idea slightly longer than my first option, but being blessed with a somewhat timid character, I simply did not dare take this approach, at least not so early in my first year. That left only one remaining option. I would simply pick an especially good day, wait until about 3:20, and walk right into Mr. Koning's office and ask permission to leave early to do a little duck hunting on my way home. There was nothing to lose.

Well, the appointed day came, and gradually my nerve began to take leave. Mr. Koning didn't seem to be in a particularly jovial mood. What kind of reaction would he have to my bold request?

The 3:15 bell clanged, and kids rushed to their lockers. The halls were empty by 3:20, so I closed my briefcase, flipped my lights off, and headed for the office. This was ridiculous; I was a grown man with one simple request, yet my heart was going nuts, and my palms were sweating almost as much as if I were already seeing mallards cupping into my decoys.

I reached the main office and noticed that Mr. Koning's door was closed. Light seeped out underneath, so I knew he was in there. What if he was in conference with another teacher? Or a board member? Maybe I'd better forget about it. No, this is it! I knocked on the door. Mr. Koning's baritone voice immediately resounded.

"Come in!"

With a trembling hand, I twisted the doorknob and entered his room . . . only to see Al standing behind his desk, bent over and struggling to pull up a pair of chest waders, a camouflaged hat already perched on his head.

"What do you need, Mr. Pluimer? Make it quick if you can—I'm heading out to the slough for a little duck hunting!"

I lost my fear of Mr. Koning that afternoon, and I gained a life-long duck hunting partner. I also learned one valuable lesson, namely that God places the right people in our paths at just the right time in our lives. Not only for opportune duck hunts, but also for our spiritual growth. Oh, sure, some of our meetings may be "chance encounters," but in many cases the people we interact with are placed in our world to serve a purpose in our spiritual walk. And God is counting on us to enact a similar influence in their lives.

Ecclesiastes 4:9–12:

Two are better than one, because they have a good return for their work; if one falls down, his friend can help him up. But pity the man who falls and has no one to help him up!

Also, if two lie down together, they will keep warm. But how can one keep warm alone? Though one may be overpowered, two can defend themselves. A cord of three strands is not quickly broken.

THE BABY LOON

The common loon, definitely mis-named since there is absolutely nothing common about it, singularly defines the Northwoods. New York City has its infamous taxi cabs, Colorado its awesome ski slopes, and Minnesota has its loons. Absent from Southern Minnesota, this courtly bird, numbering in the 10–15,000 range, graces our clear Northern lakes and serenades us at night with its haunting wail. More loons call Minnesota home than all the other states combined, with the exception of Alaska. This is the ultimate state bird, similar to the ring-necked pheasant in South Dakota; both define the character of their respective states.

On "our" lake, Clough Lake, we have at least one pair of loons each summer. This past year was special because, for the first time in five years, our pair had young—two of them in fact; typical gray fuzzballs who spent their days trailing the parents around the lake. Years ago, we seemed to have young loons each year, but for the past five seasons, our adults have not produced viable offspring. So it was with unusual pleasure that Sheri and I watched these babies grow and change. Every day the four loons would swim along our shoreline, and we would watch the parents patiently feed small minnows to the dependent little ones. For three weeks we enjoyed observing the family, and in fact we looked forward each day to spotting the family as they made their way down our shoreline.

Then one Sunday morning I awoke, went down to the kitchen to make coffee, and as I glanced out the picture window, I saw a single baby loon just outside our dock. I wondered what it was doing away from its parents at such a young age. In addition, something didn't look quite "normal" about this bird. Even though it was only 40 yards from the cabin, I dug out the binoculars to investigate. Sure enough, it was a loon all right, but something was strange. It was sopping wet, its matted feathers plastered to its body. Normally a water bird can dive and ascend, looking as dry as if it were encased in a protective plastic bubble. Not this one. It became obvious that the bird was sick or injured. I walked down to the dock, and it was then I noticed both parents and the other little one emerge from the rushes farther down the shoreline. The abnormal loon quickly swam away from me toward its parents, and I harbored the hope that perhaps it was all right after all.

One of the parents nudged the wet baby, then simply turned and swam out into the lake, soon to be joined by its mate and the healthy baby. The sick loon sank lower into the water, swam toward me and up to shore . . . and eventually died.

Sher and I watched the entire scenario unfold within a matter of minutes, and even today I cannot shake from my mind the image of that one helpless, hapless loon making its final journey right before my eyes—long before it ever had a chance to experience life's mysteries and uncertainties.

I really don't know what happened. Both young loons seemed healthy for three weeks; both energetic gray fuzzballs that eventually learned to dive and swim underwater. But one—this one—either became injured or grew sick and apparently lost the ability to protect its plumage with oil. The mishap turned out to be fatal.

I believe it is often unwise to engage in anthropomorphism, because if we did, life would be a constant progression of melancholy events. On the other hand, I don't think we can assume that other life forms have no feelings; I am convinced that some type of grieving must occur among wildlife.

What Sheri and I witnessed probably is not all that unusual, and I'm still not clear about precisely what took place. But apparently the parent loons, normally extremely protective of their young, recognized that something was terribly, fatally wrong with this little one, and they delivered it to us, or to our dock, then abandoned it to die alone. We've watched the remaining three loons daily as they press on, going about their lives without so much as a backward glance at our shoreline where one of their own spent its last minutes.

I keep analyzing this scene, and think there has to be some sermon material for our son Mark, who is in seminary. I will leave the creativity up to him, but in the meantime I am so thankful my heavenly Father does not abandon me, nor will He *ever* leave me, in spite of any circumstance I might encounter. I have the promise from Scripture that if I should develop a fatal illness, if I should become mortally injured, if I should acquire some horrific deformity—one that would cause all other humans to stare in horror and choose to leave me—no matter, God will never ever abandon me. He will never give up hope for me and leave me to my own defenses.

That gives me immense comfort. But I still feel sad for that baby loon.

Psalm 27:7–10:

Hear my voice when I call, O Lord; be merciful to me and answer me. My heart says of you, "Seek his face!"

Your face, Lord, I will seek. Do not hide your face from me, do not turn your servant away in anger; you have been my helper. Do not reject me or forsake me, O God my Savior. Though my father and mother forsake me, the Lord will receive me.

OPEN WATER

It hasn't been a particularly harsh winter, at least by Minnesota standards, but when the windchill factor is an integral part of each day's weather forecast, it has been long enough. For months now, headlights have been necessary by 5 p.m., and what precious sunlight does appear during daylight hours lacks the power to do any serious melting. Mercifully, the evenings of Scrabble in front of the fire are history (Sheri usually emerged the victor). I haven't seen an oriole or heard the gentle lapping of waves on a shoreline for five full moons, and the only throttle in my right hand has been that of my snowblower; I'm ready for an outboard. It is definitely time for a change in seasons.

For prudence' sake, we are not to constantly dwell in the future; life teaches us to live each day fully. Nevertheless, I consider it a great blessing from God to own a zest for living, an excited anticipation of things to come. For those of us living in the Northland, there is always the next season to look forward to—and it is markedly different from the present one.

I remember visiting my sister and her husband in Florida one Easter. Each morning when I awoke and stepped outside into the 72 degree sunshine, I was amazed. Mary responded, "It's always like this; we call it JAP-DIP: Just Another Perfect Day In Paradise!"

Well, in Minnesota the weather is paramount, also, because in its extremes, it dictates our outdoor activities, and it never tires of changing our plans. Right now I am reminded that winter finally seems to be relinquishing its grip on our lives; there have been subtle signs for several weeks. A stray robin or two, and finally troops of them, have been strutting across the backyard, heads cocked earthward for an unlucky earthworm. The first pitch-black pocket gopher mounds have appeared in the drab, lifeless road ditches; the frost must be receding. Last Sunday we even saw a handful of bluebirds flitting around the junipers; apparently the sun's rays have awakened the resident insect population. Weeks ago the first wedges of magnificent Canada geese drifted over our roof, bucking a fierce north wind.

All these prophets of spring set the heart to throbbing just a little faster in Minnesota, yet none of them truly heralds the spring season. That singular distinction goes to the main event of the year: *Ice out!*

The sheer exhilaration elicited by this one phrase can only be appreciated by one living in the North Country. Folks residing in more southern climes are fortunate enough to be able to slide a boat into open water 12 months of the year, making the activity something less than special. But up here we've been frozen in for six months, so when we finally get an opportunity to slide the boat onto a lake's glassy surface, it is pure magic.

Last spring, it was late April before Sheri and I launched my pike boat into the chilly water of Lake Andrew one day after school. Andrew is always our first lake of the spring, mainly out of tradition, but also because it has a healthy population of crappies that will be concentrated in a relatively small area, giving us a better chance of finding them.

The north shore of Andrew holds a small bay surrounded by cattails. The entire bay has a depth of only five feet, and it is this area that attracts the first schools of crappies. Contrary to popular belief, they are not visiting the bay to spawn; with 40 degree water temperatures, that ritual is still weeks away. But this bay has the warmest water in the lake, which means its insect life and other invertebrate life will awaken early. Winter usually brings sparse feeding opportunities for panfish, so in the spring, the insect larvae are welcome sustenance.

Sheri and I endured the bone-chilling ride across the lake and soon reached the protection, quiet, and relative warmth of the north bay. I killed the 90 horsepower Johnson, drifted into the glassy bay, then walked to the bow and swung the electric motor into the water. It was anybody's guess where the crappies might be, if they were here at all. So our plan was to slowly motor around the bay, casting to docks, brush piles, overhanging trees, and anything else that may provide some cover for the fish.

I selected two tiny leadhead jigs of different colors and tied one on each of our lines. After attaching a small pencil bobber to each line, I impaled a small crappie minnow onto each jig. We then began casting. Oh, it felt so good!

As we slowly worked our way along the shoreline, the year's first Baltimore oriole poured out its sweet melody from high in a cottonwood tree, the flashy orange of the male in stark contrast with the fresh lime green leaves of a new season.

A pair of wood-ducks did a close fly-by of our boat, their whistles eerily echoing across the bay.

A wedge of black, fish-eating cormorants crept across the blue sky northward, and I vocally urged them to keep going, to head someplace else to wreak their havoc.

The faint aroma of gasoline and exhaust fumes wafted across the water as a reminder of past days on the lake.

The delicious smell of burning leaves and grass hung over the water; someone on the west shore was raking their yard and burning the evidence.

We had plenty of time to soak up these sensations, for the fishing was excruciatingly slow. Well, the fishing was great, but the catching was non-existent. I always expect that on the first trip. It seems the water is just too cold yet, and the schools of crappies are scattered all over the big lake. Nevertheless, we set out each spring with heightened anxiety and anticipation. Catching fish is not of paramount significance; simply experiencing open water is enough.

By the time we'd reached the far eastern shore of the bay, where the water was the shallowest, my thermometer registered seven degrees warmer than in the main lake. We began encountering a few fish. Four times in the span of 15 minutes, a bobber slowly disappeared under the clear water's surface. Each time, a gentle hookset resulted in a fat, black slab of a crappie, each of them 10–12 inches. This certainly was no summertime walleye bonanza, but after five months of iced up lakes, the throbbing little ultralight rod felt fabulous!

Before we finished, Sheri and I even hit a bonus—we ran into a school of largemouth bass that had also found their way into the bay, and they were hungry! Crappie minnows served as dessert for the marauding bass, and for awhile, every single cast resulted in either a missed fish or a powerful fight on light tackle. Bass season was still six weeks away, but we were legitimately fishing crappies. We couldn't help it if some suicidal bass wanted to sample our lures!

This is spring in Minnesota. It doesn't offer the flush of a wild game bird before the gun; it doesn't allow for the observation of a magnificent whitetail buck under the tree stand. Nor will it permit an angler to pitch plastic worms along a deep weedline in search of largemouths. But it offers open water and a fresh start to another season. We tend to appreciate more those things we do not always have. Only God fully realizes how much we relish that first spring-time trip onto open water.

1 Timothy 6:17–19:

Command those who are rich in this present world not to be arrogant nor to put their hope in wealth, which is so uncertain, but to put their hope in God, who richly provides us with everything for our enjoyment. Command them to do good, to be rich in good deeds, and to be generous and willing to share. In this way they will lay up treasure for themselves as a firm foundation for the coming age, so that they may take hold of the life that is truly life.

THE ULTIMATE GAME BIRD

Speculating about the Creation account is little more than just that—speculating. The book of Genesis provides a very accurate account, though scant in details. The fact of the matter is, we know for absolute certainty that God created life in the beginning. Precisely when, how, and to what extent this miraculous event transpired will likely never be determined this side of the grave. But, as I tell my students, those are just a couple of the many questions I plan to ask God when I see Him.

Even though the Creation details are lacking, we are free to wonder, and my heart tells me it was a brilliant October day when God created aspens, tamaracks, and tag alders. I'm guessing there was a spicy, pungent odor in the air, and maybe even a hint of sweet birch wood smoke. All of creation was awash in splendor. Then, as a climax, God reached down and carefully placed a drumming ruffed grouse in the midst of the spectacular foliage He had just formed. I believe He then leaned back, smiled a little, and proclaimed, "This is my best work yet."

I have had the privilege of hunting a variety of game birds in my time, from the diminutive bob-white quail and the darting mourning dove to the giant Canada goose. Any bird on the wing can be a challenge to the gunner. Yet there is none I would rather hunt in October than the ruffed grouse. Very few sportsmen would argue with the claim that the grouse is the ultimate game bird. A delicacy on the dinner table? Yes. Physical beauty? Definitely. And, most of all, a challenging sporting target? No question.

I still remember my first grouse. In fact, I can picture the exact spot where it came to rest. I was a blossoming young hunter at the time, reading every fin and feather magazine I could lay hands on, even though I had little opportunity to indulge in my fantasies. For a year, I had been saving paper route money, and when I had finally accumulated enough, I went down to the local hardware store and picked out my first shotgun, a Winchester 16 gauge single shot. I chose a Winchester because in 1961, I figured it was the best brand out there; I chose a single shot because, at the time, it was all I could afford.

In the months that followed, my actual hunting experience was limited, but my enthusiasm was not. Consequently when four sporting adults from our church invited me along on a grouse hunt one Saturday, I was ecstatic. I tossed and turned the entire night before the hunt; each time I opened my eyes to squint at the alarm clock, the soft rays from the street light illuminated the gear lying in a neat pile on the floor alongside my bed: hunting clothes, boots, a box of shells and my prized new shotgun.

The hunt itself proved to be everything a grouse hunt usually is—a mosaic of brilliant woodland colors, pungent fall odors, plenty of explosive flushes, and for me, utter futility. That Winchester 16 gauge, with its shiny bluing and rich walnut stock, was my treasure. Little did I know that it would serve me so poorly that day—in no small part due to my inexperience at hitting anything on the move, but also due to the long 32 inch barrel and full choke and its propensity for wickedly punching my shoulder each time I pulled the trigger. As the day wore on and the other four guys were experiencing moderate success, I was having trouble even getting off a shot, much less connecting with a rocketing ruffed grouse. It seemed that every time a grouse exploded from the underbrush in front of me, the bird was but a fleeting memory by the time my gun was shouldered. I had never imagined grouse hunting to be so difficult and so frustrating.

Then early in the afternoon, it happened. Scarcely fifty feet in front of me, strutting on a fallen log, was *my* grouse. How I managed to see him through the dense brush is a mystery, but there he was, big, boastful, and *mine*. I slipped the gun to my shoulder, pulled the hammer back, took a quick bead, and squeezed the trigger. A cloud of feathers erupted as my prize was bowled off its perch.

"I got him!" I shouted as I beat my way through the underbrush to claim my trophy. Upon hearing my exclamation, the other guys all hurried over to congratulate me and share in my glory. There I stood, proudly hoisting my bird up and examining it—my first ruffed grouse! Around me lay a ring of feathers marking the spot where the bird had been blown off its perch. One of the men nonchalantly mentioned that by the looks of all the feathers, this bird wasn't far off the ground when my shot tumbled him. I innocently admitted that, no, he sure wasn't and that in fact I'd shot him right off the log.

The congratulations and frivolity suddenly ceased. The woods became strangely silent. My grin faded as I sensed something was wrong. Then one of the men simply said, "If you *ever* shoot a bird on the ground again, it'll be your last hunt with us. Don't forget that!"

I never did forget it, and I've never since swatted a bird on the ground. That single, powerful lesson humiliated me so severely that day that I was driven to tears. But the lesson stuck, and I wish all aspiring young hunters could experience such a powerful lesson early in their hunting careers. Perhaps it would cause them to reflect on their reasons for hunting, and perhaps it would help them understand, admire, and appreciate their quarry more.

Birds are a renewable resource, and I believe God gave them to us for our use and enjoyment. They are to be treasured and respected. All game birds should be treated with the dignity they deserve. To blast one on the ground or from a tree is to view it as nothing more than a piece of meat. Grouse deserve far better than that.

Genesis 1:20–25:

And God said, "Let the water teem with living creatures, and let birds fly above the earth across the expanse of the sky."

So God created the great creatures of the sea and every living and moving thing with which the water teems, according to their kinds, and every winged bird according to its kind. And God saw that it was good. God blessed them and said, "Be fruitful and increase in number and fill the water in the seas, and let the birds increase on the earth." And there was evening and there was morning—the fifth day.

And God said, "Let the land produce living creatures according to their kinds: livestock, creatures that move along the ground, and wild animals, each according to its kind." And it was so. God made the wild animals according to their kinds, the livestock according to their kinds, and all the creatures that move along the ground according to their kinds. And God saw that it was good.

THE STATE RECORD

The entire shoreline of Horseshoe Lake bristles with docks. Their variety boggles the mind; some are short, while some project 200 feet into the lake; some are constructed of wood, others of metal. A few of the newer ones are even made of fiberglass. But all of them sport a boat or two moored to them, and these structures represent shade and cover. And on Horseshoe, where there is shade there is bound to be a largemouth bass. Or two or three.

These human walkways are so numerous and in such close proximity to each other that, from the lake, fishermen identify them not by pointing to them, but by describing the boats they support. "The dock on the west shore with the big Skeeter." Or "the new fiberglass dock with the Sylvan deckboat sporting a new Honda 90."

At any rate, for my son Mark, all these docks jumble together in anonymity with the exception of one. There is a dock on the west shore of the first basin whose every detail is etched into Mark's memory. Even ten years from now, if that dock is still there, he will be able to take you directly to it, and in fact will likely point out one specific corner of the dock. That dock held the new Minnesota state record largemouth. Maybe. And she was Mark's. Almost. And he'll never forget her. Ever.

One afternoon in August, Mark decided he needed a fishing break. Since there was no-one available to accompany him, he hitched up his 14 foot Lund to his truck and summoned our black Lab Lexus to join him. Lex has been Mark's puppy from the very first day we got her, and she likes nothing better than being at Mark's side, whether it be in a duck blind, a piece of pheasant cover, or even in a fishing boat.

And so it was that Mark set out on this particular day to try to lure a few bass away from the docks on Horseshoe Lake. He fished for about an hour and caught eight bass, most of which were on the small side. He was having a good time, enjoying a sunny, calm afternoon with Lexus, daydreaming and relaxing. Then it happened. Mark had used his electric motor to ease up to a long dock with an "L" at the end and a pontoon tied to each side. He had flipped his lure to the corner of the dock, where the shade from one of the pontoons projected five feet out into the lake. Instantly, a "boil" erupted on the surface, and Mark set the hook. The eight-pound monofilament stretched tight, and like a locomotive the bass bored for deep water, straight out from the dock. Within a flash, it was all over. Mark recalled that he had produced a good hookset and had full pressure on the big fish, but all of the sudden the line went limp, a giant swirl appeared on the surface of the water 50 feet away, and he reeled in his lure. He had been throwing a 7" Berkley Power Worm rigged Texas style on a 1/8 oz sliderhead. Mark said when he retrieved his lure to re-rig his worm, his knees began shaking. The 2/0 Gamakatsu hook had twisted almost 180 degrees until it resembled a straight pin. What kind of fish was this?

Once he regained his composure, Mark started his Johnson outboard and slowly cruised away; he would let that dock rest and come back to it later. Most likely that behemoth bass would move out someplace and sulk, but when you lose a fish like this, you cannot help but revisit the fateful spot time and again, each time eternally optimistic that the brute is still there. For almost an hour, Mark absent-mindedly fished several other docks, faithfully casting his lure to every shady nook and cranny. But truthfully, he couldn't shake the memory and the feel of that big bass.

Finally, he cruised back to the same dock, approaching it from a different direction, and cut his gas motor while still 50 yards out into the lake. Silently, he slipped closer, into casting range, then carefully flipped a newly rigged Power Worm into the same corner where he'd encountered the fish earlier. Again, the water exploded, and Mark reared back with a powerful hookset, driving the barb home. It was the same fish! The huge bass wallowed on the surface, giving Mark a quick but good glimpse, but instead of heading for deep water, it bored further under the dock. Mark's line cut through the water, then abruptly stopped, still taut. All of Mark's strength had not been able to turn the fish, and it wrapped around one of the dock posts.

Frantically, Mark hit "high" on his electric motor and moved in to free the fish. Knees knocking, palms sweating, he maneuvered the boat closer . . . and then with a sickening flick of its tail, the big bass snapped the line and for a brief instant lay there in full view, not realizing it was free. Mark said the scene unfolded in slow motion, and to this day he still sees that "state record" fish slide tauntingly back under the dock. Grown men seldom cry. But big bass force men to do things they normally wouldn't. For five minutes Mark sat, dejected, sick to his stomach. It was over. There was nothing left to do but go home. Additional fishing was out of the question. No other bass could compare, and this one was gone.

Was it truly a Minnesota state record? One over eight pounds, 15 ounces? Probably not. But Mark is a very experienced bass angler, having guided for a couple summers, and has caught bass of six pounds and has been present in the boat with bass of seven pounds. He knows big fish, and he got a close look at this one. Regardless, it was gone, and no matter how many times Mark or I have pulled up to that secret dock with hopes higher than an eagle on a thermal, we've never encountered Grandma again.

True fishermen are eternally optimistic. Each day they embark on the water, they know in their heart that today might be the day they tie into a trophy. If they succeed, then their equipment, their total skill, and a little luck all have to gel perfectly for the fish to be landed. Often a monster escapes; that is what makes it a trophy.

Fishing: It is ironic that a passion which gives so much pleasure is capable of inflicting so much inner pain. Perhaps God uses even experiences as this to temper us, strengthen us, and build character.

James 1:2–8, 12:

Consider it pure joy, my brothers, whenever you face trials of many kinds, because you know that the testing of your faith develops perseverance. Perseverance must finish its work so that you may be mature and complete, not lacking anything. If any of you lacks wisdom, he should ask God, who gives generously to all without finding fault, and it will be given to him. But when he asks, he must believe and not doubt, because he who doubts is like a wave of the sea, blown and tossed by the wind. That man should not think he will receive anything from the Lord; he is a double-minded man, unstable in all he does.

Blessed is the man who perseveres under trial, because when he has stood the test, he will receive the crown of life that God has promised to those who love him.

EVEN THE STONES WILL CRY OUT

The Scriptures proclaim that all creation sings praises to God. During Jesus' triumphal entry into Jerusalem, his disciples broke into shouts of praise for all the miracles they'd witnessed. Some of the Pharisees in the crowd grew irritated and told Jesus to shut up his disciples. His curt reply:

"I tell you, if they keep quiet the stones will cry out."

Again, the book of Isaiah tells us that if we go out into the world as followers of Jesus Christ, "the mountains and hills will burst into song before us and all the trees of the field will clap their hands."

Indeed, anyone who whiles away his time outdoors has witnessed this. In the woods, in the sloughs, in the fields, on the lakes, the sounds and sights around us bear witness to a Superior Being, the Creator of the entire universe.

Who cannot be moved at the sudden roar from the sky as a squadron of bluebills knifes earthward, rending the heavens while the deafening rush of air encounters their pinions? No other sound on Earth trips my pacemaker like this one. Or what about the sounds emanating from a duck slough in the chilly pre-dawn, after the decoys have been meticulously spread and you're hunched in your canoe, waiting for legal shooting time? As you sense the cold steel of your gun barrel through your thin gloves, you are aware of the hoarse quacking of hen mallards feeding in the duckweed and the loud nasal proclamations of dozens of blue-wing teal doing likewise. It is still too dark to see anything on the water, but all the quacking and babbling frees your mind to conjure up all sorts of images.

Or, how many times have you leaped out of bed in the middle of an April night, rushed to the open bedroom window and thrust it further open to catch the clamor of a huge flock of Canada geese passing directly over your rooftop on their northward journey? These magnificent, huge (some surpassing 15 pounds), black and white fowl have been wintering down near the Gulf and now are pulling their way up to their Canadian breeding grounds to once again fulfill the feral urge to mate and bring off another brood of goslings, thereby perpetuating that incredible species. Precisely how do they navigate? What guides them? How many miles has this flock traveled so far today? Where will they put down? How close to a particular female's hatching place will an adult pair wind up? How many seasons of blinds and BBs have they encountered, outwitted, and survived? These things and more I ponder as I crawl back under the warm sheets.

In addition to auditory sensations such as these, there are many visual stimuli that never fail to register awe in the mind of a naturalist. Wildlife calendars have created a somewhat "trite" picture of the scene, but nevertheless, the sight of brilliant greenheads cupping their wings over decoys . . . well, nothing in October can compare. Or how about an entire flock of wood-ducks suddenly "maple-leafing" from the stratosphere to rapidly lose altitude and pitch toward an overgrown back bay of a Minnesota marsh?

Picture a northern lake at sunset, its flat calm surface mirroring dark pines and red clouds, when suddenly a mammoth "boil" erupts in the lily pads just outside a towering beaver dam. In your gut you just know the receding rings on the water belong to a state record largemouth bass, and now you won't be able to sleep all night.

Even such a simple phenomenon as color should elicit our praise. Can there be anything more brilliant than a drake woodie in full breeding plumage in May? Or the russet tones of a brown thrasher flitting among the lime-green new growth of a honeysuckle hedge?

As we blend into the outdoors and become aware of the life around us, even if we do *not* express our awe or praise, nature refuses to be kept silent. All of God's creative works are such specimens of perfection and wonder that they naturally and spontaneously shout God's praises. It is a gross error in judgement, however, to think that we need not lend voice to our own musings. Just as a spouse needs to be reminded frequently, to be *told* she is loved and appreciated, so it is with our Creator. The prudent husband will not let his wife forget that he appreciates her. And that is what God desires from us; He knows the desires of our heart, He knows what we're thinking. But for us to remain silent when enjoying His handiwork is still to ignore Him, perhaps even to slap Him in the face.

You know, I cannot help wondering . . . when such natural images and sounds connect with our brain, they are eventually registered in that tiny gland called the pituitary, miniscule in size, yet so magnum in significance that it formerly was termed our master gland. Upon registering these stimuli, the anterior lobe of the pituitary secretes a hormone called ACTH, which may aid in stimulating the adrenal glands atop our kidneys to release adrenaline . . . which in turn raises our blood pressure, increases the heart rate, dilates our bronchioles and also the pupils of our eyes. In other words, the entire body is put on edge or high alert. Why is this? I suppose a case could be made that this is an evolutionary adaptation suited for our ancestors to enable them to survive an attacking saber tooth tiger. But I doubt it. More likely, it is simply that God wants us to stop, take note, and utter a *"Wow!"* of amazement when our outdoor forays lead us to an encounter with one of His creatures. After all, we don't want the stones to be the only things crying His praise.

Psalm 96:11,12:

Let the heavens rejoice, let the earth be glad; let the sea resound, and all that is in it; let the fields be jubilant, and everything in them. Then all the trees of the forest will sing for joy.

MISSED SHOTS

Every good wingshooter has a few vivid recollections of spectacular shots he has made over the years—perhaps that crossing double on mallards or a rocketing twisting grouse in thick aspen. With a little luck, there was even a witness or two to corroborate the feat. Most likely, that same shooter can also reach back into his past and call up some incredibly easy shots he has missed. Believe me; I've got some "doozies."

As a young college student, my shooting prowess earned me quite a reputation. Friends always invited me along on hunting trips because it became pretty universally known that I would miss the birds, meaning that the other members of the party could shoot more than their share in order for the party to fill out. My own personal game bag usually felt rather light.

There was the time in southern Michigan when I was pheasant hunting with three buddies and all four of us had managed several shots on roosters, but I was the only one whose shots had failed to find their mark.

Finally, a lone cock bird flushed wild ahead of my buddy's Springer spaniel, and the bird sailed safely into a patch of bedroom-sized cover 200 yards away. We promptly scurried to the spot, eyes glued to the cover. Upon drawing near, one of my more compassionate companions declared,

"Hey, this bird is Den's; he hasn't shot one yet today. Let him go in first with the dog and get the first shot. If he misses, we'll back him up."

Heart pounding, palms sweating, I carefully entered the patch of brush just as the little spaniel went very birdy. Suddenly, from under the dog's nose and scarcely 20 yards in front of me, the rooster erupted, and with a mighty leap, that little Springer neatly plucked him right out of the air. My Wingmaster had barely made its way to my shoulder. Such was my luck in those days; I didn't "miss" that easy shot, but the result was the same, anyway—an empty game bag.

A couple years later I accepted my first teaching position in northwest Iowa, a land bursting with cooperative pheasants and very forgiving of a man who can't shoot well. A hunter could afford to miss two or three birds in a day because he could still end up with a couple to take home.

One day after school, late in the season when all remaining birds were concentrated together in thick cover, I walked an impenetrable grove of conifers where it seemed as though every bird in Sioux County was roosting in the safety of the thick greenery. Getting a glimpse of the wildly flushing birds was next to impossible, but the ruckus they made as they escaped put the adrenal glands on high alert.

Near the end of the grove, I heard a raucous "cackle, cackle" and watched a big, dark bird sail out into a picked cornfield. Again, I hurried straight to the spot where I'd seen him land. The harvested cornfield was void of any cover except for the chopped stalks, so if I could flush this bird in range, he was mine. When I reached the spot where I had marked the bird, he was nowhere to be found. I couldn't believe it; where was he? Then I saw something—a long tail protruding from a twisted clump of cornstalks. I approached the clump and kicked at it. The big colorful bird jumped up and lumbered straight away from me, seemingly as big and slow as a helicopter.

I shouldered my 12 gauge Wingmaster and touched the trigger when the big bird appeared above the barrel. At the report, the bird gave no indication I had even startled it, so I pumped another shell into the chamber and fired again. I repeated that process three more times until five empty, smoking hulls lay at my feet. The rooster disappeared into the clear, blue sky, and I'm positive I heard his cackle turn into laughter after my fifth shot.

Undoubtedly, my worst performance came much later, in fact just two short seasons ago, when Mike and I were duck hunting in Wubben's Slough, just down the road from our house. The two of us had totally hidden our canoe in a thick bank of cattails overlooking our modest spread of two dozen decoys, and the normal sunrise flurry of action had not yet transpired. It was shaping up to be a gorgeous morning, but it looked as though the waterfowl may have already left for southern waters. About an hour after dawn, an unmistakable "Ha-ronk, ha-ronk!" reached our ears from the far shore of the slough—geese! Peering over the cattails, we made out four gray shapes winging their way directly toward us, scarcely ten feet off the water. If they continued their present course, they would almost collide with us! We immediately hunched down in the canoe and nervously waited, and the four Canadas kept coming.

The honking grew louder and louder, and all of the sudden, we realized the great birds were literally on top of us. I remember thinking that this was so easy, the only thing we had to concern ourselves with was to each shoot at different birds. I had no doubt we would dump all four geese. We heard wingbeats as we both stood. I cannot exaggerate the size of those birds; they were indeed giant Canada geese, the most abundant race of Canadas in the area, some of which reach 16–20 pounds. I also need not exaggerate the range; a typical bamboo cane pole could have swatted them out of the sky. As I rose, I picked out the bird farthest to my left, as Mike stood to my right. The barrel of my Browning A-5 12 gauge caught up with its head, and I touched the trigger just as I heard Mike's Remington go off. My bird never even shuddered, so I pulled another shot, then quickly swung on a different bird and fired my last shell. Mike's gun was still barking and all four geese were now safely departing, still only 30 yards away.

To this day, Mike and I still talk about that morning and just shake our heads. We don't have a clue where we shot or how we could have possibly missed those four huge targets at that range. I suppose they were actually too close for our shotguns to throw a decent pattern, but one would think that at least by the third shot, we would have connected. The only bright spot to the story is that Wubben's Slough was empty of all other hunters that morning, so there was nobody to witness our debacle. (Ironically, just five minutes later, a diminutive green wing teal the size of a softball strafed the outer perimeter of our decoy spread, and Mike calmly centered it and killed it cleanly with one shot. A dozen teal just like it could easily fit into the space occupied by one Canada goose.

And then there was that unbelievably easy ruffed grouse shot last fall . . . no, this time I'm lying. Oh, I've missed my share of grouse, and then some. But there's no such thing as an easy grouse shot. If there ever was one, though, I'm confident I could blow that one, also.

Isaiah 66:1,2:

This is what the Lord says:

"Heaven is my throne, and the earth is my footstool. Where is the house you will build for me?

Where will my resting place be? Has not my hand made all these things, and so they came into being?" declares the Lord.

"This is the one I esteem: he who is humble and contrite in spirit, and trembles at my word."

LARGEMOUTH WALLEYES

It was a late afternoon in mid July at the end of a successful guide trip on Lake Ada. We had fished two lakes, finishing on Ada, where I had figured the action would be a little slower than on the first lake, but where the fish would be bigger. Both guesses turned out to be true, and we had a few nice fish sloshing around in the livewell during the ride back to the public access. Not a spectacular day, but a satisfying one for both me and my clients, especially in mid July, arguably the toughest fishing month of the summer.

The humidity was high and the sun hot, so the 40 mph race across the waves felt refreshing and rewarding. I turned through the narrows on the north end of the lake and shot toward the access, where I quickly throttled down and glided toward the dock.

I was disappointed to see another trailer in the water on the cement ramp, as I didn't relish the idea of idling under the hot sun. We waited in place for a minute or so until I realized the guy standing alongside the trailer seemed to be making no progress. Noticing the license plate on the trailer was from Indiana, I figured I'd go up to the guy and strike up a conversation; may as well promote Minnesota fishing whenever possible.

I beached my boat, hopped out, and ambled toward the trailer, where the guy had his back toward me. He didn't seem to be in any hurry to load his boat. Then I noticed the fish cleaning board resting on his trailer and saw a fillet knife in his hand. He was cleaning fish of all things! At least he could load up his boat first so other anglers wouldn't be left waiting.

I announced my presence: "Howdy! How's fishin'?"

"Well, it's been pretty good, but now our vacation is over and we have to head back home," the man replied.

"But you had good fishing?" I inquired again, always eager to find specific fishing information that may help me in my business.

"Yeah, well this was our first trip to Lake Ada, but we did okay."

"What kind of fish did you get?" I asked further.

"Both northerns and walleyes. The folks at the resort said the walleyes taste better, so we've been throwing the northerns back and just eating the walleyes."

Now two statements he made set me off. First of all, I am one of those in the vast minority of Minnesotans who prefers eating northern over walleye. It is my opinion that if you can get the "Y" bones out of a northern fillet, you'll have the best tasting fish around. But what really turned my crank was the guy's statement about their walleye success. I fish Ada frequently, mostly for northerns, but never for walleyes. The walleyes in Ada are very difficult to come by except through the ice. And now this foreigner from Indiana who had never fished the lake before had caught walleyes all week. I don't mind admitting that my pride was wounded.

"What did you take them on?" I boldly asked.

"Nightcrawlers," came the reply. That made sense to me—summer time walleyes and crawlers go together. But now I grew even more frustrated. I enjoy running a live-bait rig with a crawler along a sandy bottom for summer 'eyes. But Lake Ada's heavy, healthy cabbage and coontail weedlines made running a live-bait rig very difficult. In fact, I get totally discouraged every time I try it. How was this guy fishing his live-bait rig?

I decided to draw closer and see what other information I could pick up. Often one can gain some valuable hints just by noticing the terminal tackle rigged up in someone else's boat. The guy stood up to straighten his back after being bent over his fish cleaning board, and I observed a five gallon bucket resting on the other side of the trailer. I peered down into the bucket—and saw three fair sized largemouth bass floating belly-up.

"Oh, you caught some bass also, huh?" I asked, now more disturbed than ever. I had promoted catch and release for bass for two decades, long before the practice was in vogue.

"No, no bass. Just these here walleyes!"

Well, as they say, it takes all kinds, and I'm certainly not going to judge all Hoosiers based on the ignorance of this particular fisherman, but I know this: Minnesota is a walleye-crazed state, and that fish is often pursued as if it had mythological, magical powers. If I could convince my customers that the 2000 bass they catch each summer are walleyes instead, I'd likely be the most sought after guide in the state.

In the book of James we learn that Jesus had very strong opinions about those who treat people based on their "status." Some folks consider bass as "trash" fish while walleyes are placed on a graphite pedestal. The Indiana fisherman was feeling good about his fishing prowess until he learned his catch was made up of bass rather than walleyes. His bobber had been totally burst.

Now, by no means am I suggesting it is a sin to prefer walleyes over bass. Many of my walleye buddies would want to drape an anchor around my neck and drop me overboard were I to make that proclamation. But sometimes we impart the same logic to humans as we do to fish, so we treat people differently according to their professions or their material wealth. That, says God, is a sin.

James 2:2–4,9:

Suppose a man comes into your meeting wearing a gold ring and fine clothes, and a poor man in shabby clothes also comes in. If you show special attention to the man wearing fine clothes and say, "Here's a good seat for you," but say to the poor man, "You stand there" or "Sit on the floor by my feet," have you not discriminated among yourselves and become judges with evil thoughts?

But if you show favoritism, you sin and are convicted by the law as lawbreakers.

THAT'S WHY THEY CALL IT HUNTING
RATHER THAN SHOOTING

I've been hunting for over 35 years, so it is only logical that my hunting attitude has undergone a major metamorphosis. In my early years, success was measured by the heft of my game bag. Needless to say, my success was rather infrequent. Now, with 35 years' experience at my backside, I realize that many of my most "unsuccessful" hunts have in reality been very good hunts. It all depends on perspective.

The fall of '99 seemed to generate more than a few seemingly unsuccessful hunts. In mid November, I spent many afternoons after school tramping through the sloughs in the Waterfowl Production Areas around home. My excuse for such activity is that, for me, it represents "stress reduction." Every job brings its own particular stress, and with mine it is freshmen. They happen to be a tad bit young and immature for my taste; by the time they reach their sophomore year, I can tolerate them, and if I survive to see their junior and senior years, most of them are downright lovable. At any rate, during the fall months, even a half hour of hunting after school can drain away all my tension.

This particular fall had been unusually mild, so there was no such thing as tracking birds in snow. In fact, the temperatures were well above normal all month and precipitation below normal; the sloughs were beginning to dry up. The pheasant season was in its fourth week, meaning all the young juvenile roosters (read "dumb") had already been harvested. After all, these were public hunting areas that see small armies of orange-clad hunters on weekends. Any surviving roosters knew better than to hang out in the knee-high grass they frequented in October; security now was to be found in the heavy, dense cattails out in the slough.

On one particular day, I let Lexus out of the truck, loaded my Browning Over/Under and proceeded to work the perimeter of a big slough. I had one hour of daylight, just enough to work my way around the slough and end up back at the truck by sunset, provided the dog did not go into overtime with bird encounters. Lex and I hunted fifteen minutes before she gave even a hint that the slough held any life. The ultra dry conditions meant it was next to impossible for a dog to pick up any scent. All of the sudden, Lex's tail gave her away; she was working on a bird. She zigged and zagged the cattails in front of me for about a minute, frantically trying to pin down the scent that was her whole reason for existence. Suddenly she made a cast toward open water, weaving her way through the cover. I followed on a trot until I hit the heavier cattails, then began bullying my way through the tall stuff, pausing frequently to listen for the dog.

Wherever Lexus dug her way through the cattails, the dry, loose flowers were released into the air, so it was not at all difficult to "see" where she was. I kept going, even as the water rose over my ankles. Lexus was growing "hotter" (I could tell by the commotion in the cattails), but finally I decided I couldn't go any further. Then a bird erupted 20 yards in front of me, right in front of the dog, then another, then one behind me. I swung on each one, but there was no color, no cackling, no rooster. I was disappointed, but mostly for my Lab; she had done her duty, and I had not rewarded her.

Determined, I pushed on. It was apparent the pheasants were all seeking refuge in the denser cover. I would just have to work them. The dog and I continued to trudge the slough, and soon the 75 degree temperature had me drenched in perspiration. Fuzzy cattail flowers adorned my wet face. Stout stems frequently poked me in the groin or thigh. Several times I hit wet holes deeper than my hunting boots, and my feet became soaked. Frustration eventually set in; hunting cattails was *work!* This was no longer as much fun as I had remembered. Finally, nearing the end of the slough, with the huge red sun perched on the horizon, Lexus got excited once more, and began working still deeper into the cover, sloshing through the water. Already wet, I followed. I pushed harder, breaking down the growth in front of me, but soon I couldn't keep up with the excited Lab. A raucous "cackle, cackle" brought me to a stop as I threw the safety off and shouldered my 12 gauge. Over the cattails I glimpsed the bird—a huge, brilliantly colored cock bird with a long tail. The two foot tail was curled and dangling because it was sopping wet; that bird had actually been running in water before he erupted 50 yards in front of me, leaving a very marginal shot. I lowered my gun, disappointed. The rooster had jumped at the fringe of my range, and even if I'd managed to scratch it down, the cover out there was so heavy that even Lexus may never find it. The bird deserved a better fate than that. The hunt was over. I was tired, beat, sweaty, and worn out. And I hadn't fired a single shot. The lone rooster I'd seen had outsmarted me.

Ironically, two days later, as the next weekend approached, my son and I decided to head up to the cabin for some grouse hunting. Ruffed grouse hunting is not the logical choice for a means at redeeming one's poor hunting fortunes, as these birds are arguably the most difficult targets of all North American game birds. Nevertheless, Mike and I needed some "R&R" time in the November woods. Granted, the grouse season had been open for two months, so there would not be as many birds around, but the conditions were prime: all the foliage had disappeared, and if a grouse flushed within 50 yards, we'd likely see it—perhaps only a fleeting glimpse of brown feathers, but at least our shooting chances would be greater than in September.

And so it was on this November day, with dead leaves crunching underfoot and all the smells of the Northwoods permeating our being, we set out to bag a grouse or two, and my hopes were high. By late afternoon, my hopes were waning measurably. We'd walked about six miles, and six miles of grouse cover is at least a dozen miles on typical terrain. My knees were sore, my ankles ached I was sweating profusely from bucking through brambles and prickly ash. My hands were scratched raw, I'd been poked in the eye once, slapped in the face twice by ambushing branches, and my game bag was suspiciously light. Oh, we had had flushes. Fourteen if I recall. My shell vest held four fewer shells than when I'd begun, but most of those shots were "hope shots." One soon learns that with grouse, you'd better shoot quickly and instinctively, even if the shot is partially obstructed. There is *never* an easy grouse shot.

Nevertheless, I should have had two birds in the bag. The "easiest" chance of the entire season came when Mike flushed a big brown-phase bird 50 yards to my right and hollered to me as it streaked through the woods in my direction. I swung my shotgun as the bird practically collided with my hat, wisely decided not to shoot, and spun around to intercept the bird as it veered away from me. I caught a glimpse of feathers over my barrel and touched off a shot, then another. Two large popple trees paid the price. That bird—coincidentally or instinctively—darted behind the two trees and then flew in a straight line away from me. I never saw it again after I pulled the trigger the first time.

Such a typical sight for me: Over/Under cracked open, barrels smoking, two empty shell cases lying in the leaves at my feet. A few leaves or shards of bark wafting gently earthward from where my errant pellets hit, and I'm left with a multitude of excuses to choose from in this particular instance. In any case, there's no downed bird.

And so it was, within one week I had had the privilege of hunting both ring-neck pheasants and ruffed grouse. I had researched my quarry thoroughly, and I had worked hard and put in long hours working heavy cover. At the end of each hunt, I was left with an empty game bag, as a bird with a brain the size of a pea had gotten the best of me.

Frustrating? Not really. God has granted me the means and the opportunity to spend hours afield. Better yet, He has fashioned some birds totally deserving of the title "game bird." Furthermore, every once in awhile, all facets of the hunt gel perfectly: my dog actually flushes a legal bird in range, my reactions are adequate, and pellets and bird reach a common spot at the same time. Sher and I treasure that bird over rice. That is a special gift. But if my hunt produces no bird . . . well, praise God for that, also!

Revelation 4:11:

You are worthy, our Lord and God, to receive glory and honor and power, for you created all things, and by your will they were created and have their being.

THE FISH HAWK'S LESSON

Our Creator has stockpiled planet Earth with abundant pleasures that are free for the taking—if we only break from our frantic race through life to notice them. Sunrises, sunsets, bursting milkweed pods, migrating Monarchs, stunning cloud formations, flaming sumac in September—our immediate world brims with natural beauty and wonder.

When was the last time you pulled your car over onto the shoulder to take in the awesome fuchsia, orange, and indigo of an autumn sunset? When you did, did the thought cross your mind that just maybe God was painting that sky solely for you at that moment? Oh, I know—any given sunset can be viewed and enjoyed by thousands of people at once, so the notion that your Father was projecting that color slide on the western screen just for your benefit may sound a little presumptuous. On the other hand, to deny that He had you in mind when He began the painting may be a greater error. I prefer to think that God is busy creating memorable moments for me, and that as long as I continue to enjoy those daily natural spectacles and pause long enough to give Him the praise and glory, my life will continue to be enriched.

We humans often tend to take for granted those "precious moments" simply because they occur so often. It is the fleeting, the transient, that we dote upon. I suppose if a brilliant sunset lasted an hour, we wouldn't appreciate it so much.

I remember early in my guiding career, so many of my customers from Illinois, Indiana, and Iowa would vocally marvel at the stunning water clarity in north central Minnesota. The waters in their agricultural areas are muddy—a stark contrast. But my customers' comments initially caught me off guard. Had I grown so accustomed to these clean, clear waters that I no longer noticed them? That is simply a sin. I was chagrined by this realization, and it prompted me to take a fresher look at my immediate world.

It is amazing how many "God sightings" we can observe in nature if our minds are tuned to the proper frequency. A case in point: A few years ago I was guiding two young men on a bass trip on Moccasin Lake. I guide about 35 lakes, but Moccassin has been a real treasure. Minnesota's Department of Natural Resources has designated it as a Catch and Release lake for five years as an experimental project. I have found it to hold large numbers of bass, including some true trophies. Moccassin also has the distinction of being situated in the midst of the Chippewa National Forest. The surrounding scenery is spectacular, the wildlife abundant, and much of the shoreline is Federal land, therefore undeveloped. When fishing there, the impression comes easily that one is on a wilderness lake.

The Chippewa also happens to be home to the largest number of nesting bald eagle pairs outside Alaska, making them a common, daily sighting when fishing Moccassin. I never ever grow tired of sighting an eagle, nor do my customers. Both bald eagles and ospreys (fish hawks) frequent the lakes of Cass and Crow Wing Counties, they both hunt for fish, and both are delightful to watch. Though they both fish, their fishing techniques are strikingly different. An eagle will soar over a lake, circling, often going several minutes without flapping wings. When it spots its prey it will suddenly descend and swoop to the lake's surface, plucking a fish off the water without creating so much as a ripple. Seems a wet eagle is an uncomfortable eagle. The osprey, on the other hand, also can spot wounded fish from high above the lake's surface, but then will engage in a dramatic dive and will hit the fish with such force that both bird and prey end up under water. The osprey then laboriously lifts out of the water with its meal. (I charge to take people fishing, but these little biology lessons are thrown in free.)

This particular day on Moccassin, we were fishing the north bay, casting Berkley Power Tubes toward shore, then swimming them back down the weed edge. It was a perfect day, the fish were cooperating, and I was standing in the bow operating the trolling motor. All of the sudden, an osprey came into view in front of us, flared his wings, thrust out his talons, and came in for a landing on the top of a dead birch.

Dead birches are easy to spot, even in winter when no leaves are present. Their branches become very brittle and fragile at their tips, enabling the wind to easily shear them off. In fact, the branches of dead birches become so fragile, they are often dubbed "widow makers" in the north woods. I learned early in my wood-gathering career to be extremely wary when cutting down dead birches.

This osprey came in for a landing but apparently didn't brake enough, and he slammed into a tip-top branch, cracking it off with a loud snap.

The osprey flapped powerfully and flew away with a two-foot branch in its talons. I laughed, and we all got a kick out of that; it's not often we see an "accident" in nature, even though we suspect they happen all the time. Then, of all things, a few minutes later the osprey came back and repeated his performance, this time on a different birch, but with the same results. Could he have misjudged his speed again? He lifted off with yet another long branch clasped in his talons.

Amazingly, five times that osprey "crash landed" in view of our boat, each time lifting off with a sizeable branch. I may be slow to catch on, but I'm not stupid, and I finally realized we were witnessing not a mutant predator with a flawed landing technique, but a bird in the process of rebuilding or repairing its huge stick nest in some nearby tree. Think about it—landing on the ground and searching for an appropriate stick, then lifting off again is a huge expenditure of energy for a creature on top of the food chain. I feel privileged to have witnessed a fish hawk gathering nest materials in such an efficient manner. Were I not a Christian, the scene would have been interesting, perhaps even "neat." But as one of God's children, I know I was witnessing another example of the extent to which God cares for and equips his creatures. And I am one of them.

Luke 12:22–31:

Then Jesus said to his disciples: "Therefore I tell you, do not worry about your life, what you will eat; or about your body, what you will wear. Life is more than food, and the body more than clothes. Consider the ravens: They do not sow or reap, they have no storeroom or barn; yet God feeds them. And how much more valuable you are than birds! Who of you by worrying can add a single hour to his life? Since you cannot do this very little thing, why do you worry about the rest?

"Consider how the lilies grow. They do not labor or spin. Yet I tell you, not even Solomon in all his splendor was dressed like one of these. If that is how God clothes the grass of the field, which is here today , and tomorrow is thrown into the fire, how much more will he clothe you, O you of little faith! And do not set your heart on what you will eat or drink; do not worry about it. For the pagan world runs after all such things, and your Father knows that you need them. But seek his kingdom, and these things will be given to you as well.

GUARDIAN ANGELS

During 22 years of guiding, I've encountered my share of "close calls" with the weather. I've endured a relentless hail storm about a mile out on Leech Lake; I've raced a funnel cloud across sprawling Savant Lake, thankfully managing to beach the boat on a tiny island and safely sit out the storm; I cannot count the number of times a lightning storm has forced me to get off the lake and take shelter in the truck. Such a decision is always laced with uncertainty, for invariably fish turn on in the face of an approaching storm front, and often the ensuing ten or fifteen minutes yield fantastic fishing. My job is to provide exciting fishing for clients, but obviously not at the expense of their well-being. On one occasion, I thought an electrical storm was off in the distance, but when I noticed my customer's hair start to bristle and I saw tiny "sparks" racing down my graphite rod every time I lifted it above my waist, I knew I had miscalculated. Thankfully we made it to the safety of the shore without incident, but I was definitely reminded of my responsibility to my customers.

My closest brush with disaster while on the water came, not during a guide trip, but during a Canadian trip with my close friend, Pastor Mike Reitsma. We were young, relatively inexperienced, and possibly somewhat reckless, especially when fish were to be had.

We embarked upon a week-long "trip of a lifetime," a trek into northern Manitoba for giant northern pike. We had heard rumors of monstrous northerns that had hardly seen a lure and whose numbers stretched the imagination. Furthermore, they were accessible not only by float plane, but by automobile. Even after taking into consideration the prerequisite exaggerations of the rumors we'd heard, we decided the trip was one we just had to take. Stuffing tent, sleeping bags, groceries, miscellaneous clothing, and lots of heavy tackle into our small 14' aluminum boat, we set out to drive through the night on our 20 hour journey.

Cross Lake was indeed remote; within 125 miles of its shores, the well-worn pavement gave way to a dusty gravel road. One hundred twenty-five miles have never seemed so long, what with washouts, rutted shoulders, and long stretches of wash-board surfaces. But in the end, Cross Lake came close to living up to our expectations. The northerns truly were so ubiquitous and so vicious that our arms grew weary. Although the true "monsters" generally eluded us, our first two days were very rewarding, with fish between four and ten pounds everywhere. I lost count at 175 northerns boated.

Sadly, though, fishermen are always searching for bigger fish, and that goal drove us to seek out new water the third day. Up to that point, we had not ventured more than a mile or so from camp; there was no need to, for hungry northerns awaited us in every flooded bay. But on day three, we figured if we ventured farther out onto the big lake we'd encounter fish that perhaps no fishermen had discovered this summer—and they would be bigger. So, throwing another six gallon gas tank into the boat for our 25 horse Evinrude, we set out that morning with high hopes. Our lake map showed two islands out in the middle of the lake, and that became our planned destination.

On the ride out, the weather was cooperative enough, and the outboard hummed flawlessly for over an hour as we sped toward our fishing hole. Finally, Sugar Island slipped into view, and before long we were casting large spoons into the shallow log-infested bays, hooking northerns on almost every cast. Life was good!

As time progressed, however, our dreams of giant pike slowly faded. Northerns were everywhere, and they showed no hesitancy about taking our spoons, but they were no larger than those we'd experienced near camp. One 15 pound fish and another "big" one that got away kept our hopes alive, but before long we had drained the first gas tank and were into the second, so thoughts of heading back to camp began cropping up.

Unfortunately, so did the wind. The afternoon was still reasonably sunny, with no storms brewing, but the gentle eastern breeze that had pushed us all the way out to Sugar Island in the morning was now quite stiff, which we noticed every time our boat eased around the point on the north side of the island. Fishing in the shelter of the island, it was easy to dismiss thoughts of wind. We should have known better. When we finally decided it was time to head back, we stowed the tackle, put on our life jackets, and motored around the point, turning into the whitecaps. We ran only about a minute when Mike throttled back, and we looked at each other for advice. The wind was much stronger than we'd thought, and we would have to buck it the entire way. Was this safe? Did we have enough gasoline? We quickly weighed our two options: risk it right now before the wind increased in intensity or take shelter on the island for the night. Without a tent, the prospect of spending a long night at the mercy of Manitoba's famed mosquitoes and black flies quickly forced us to choose the former. Little did we know how close that decision was to being the wrong one.

Once again, Mike faced the bow into the wind and turned the throttle. The decision was made, we dared not waste gasoline while second-guessing, so there was no turning back. We began riding the waves. The little 14' boat was wide and deep, and it handled very well. But the water was growing rougher. Soon the island was hidden from view except when we crested a wave. Alternately the bow lifted high in the air, then crashed down into a trough, forcing the outboard's whining prop out of the water. With each slam into the waves, the little aluminum boat shuddered. Soon tackle boxes were floating and fishing rods were strewn everywhere. I stopped bailing water just so I could hang on with both hands. In spite of our rainsuits and the clear, sunny sky, both Mike and I were drenched. Every time the craft hesitated on top of a wave then slammed down into the next trough, I was thrown off my seat. Only by fiercely gripping the gunwales could I avoid being thrown to the floor. By now my immediate attention was turned to our gasoline supply; I noticed Mike reach down and shake the gas tank, and I was thinking the same thing he was: if we lost power for any reason and lost the ability to head directly into the waves, we were swamped. I had been praying the entire trip, and with each passing wave successfully behind us, I grew more optimistic; now this new fear reared its head, and I resumed my prayers with additional urgency. Shore looked a long way off.

For thirty more long minutes, the little Alumacraft bounced from wave to wave, and the Evinrude would have made old Ole proud, never missing a beat. As we finally drew closer to shore, Mike was able to gun the motor just a little, and then, with fifty feet or so to go, it sputtered twice, yet continued running. I leaped out into the thigh-deep water and dragged the boat up onto the sand. We both stood there, shaking, pale, exhausted, and broke down in profound thanksgiving to the Lord for sparing us. Mike lifted the gas tank, jiggled it, and we heard no sloshing. We had run on fumes!

In retrospect, our decision to return to shore from Sugar was probably a poor one. It was not a blatantly foolish choice, as we had prayed for wisdom. But we were in a very dangerous situation, and we could have avoided it. I have no doubt that God loaned us a couple of His angels to keep guard over us on that crossing. We needed them, because it was His mercy, not our wisdom, that spared us.

Psalm 91:9–16:

If you make the Most High your dwelling—even the Lord, who is my refuge—then no harm will befall you, no disaster will come near your tent. For he will command his angels concerning you to guard you in all your ways; they will lift you up in their hands, so that you will not strike your foot against a stone.

You will tread upon the lion and the cobra; you will trample the great lion and the serpent. "Because he loves me," says the Lord, "I will rescue him; I will protect him, for he acknowledges my name. He will call upon me, and I will answer him; I will be with him in trouble, I will deliver him and honor him. With long life will I satisfy him and show him my salvation.

IN PRAISE OF GRAVEL ROADS

Who could imagine that I would be one to sing the praises of gravel roads? By summer's end, I tend to curse them rather than extol their virtues. During my summer guide trips, I log roughly 6,000 miles on my boat trailer, many of them on the roughest, dustiest gravel roads in Minnesota. It seems that up here there are very few "smooth" gravel roads, as they all share that same quirky characteristic we call the "washboard" effect, which in essence transforms a perfectly normal gravel road into one long rumble strip. I take pride in maintaining my truck and boat and keeping them looking clean and running well, but that is a fruitless task when living up North. Sometimes when I'm winding down the four mile road to Oxyoke Lake, it seems that every nut and bolt on my trailer is ready to shake loose, and weekly I develop brand new irritating rattles in the truck.

Nevertheless, gravel roads do possess a certain charm because they signal solitude, sometimes even wildness. I've never found a good grouse covert with highway access; freeways do not lead to a productive duck slough; and up here, if a lake is reached by a paved road, then it's a fairly sure bet it will host as many jet-skiers and water-skiers as fish.

There is bitter irony here—the most treasured, unspoiled wild areas are those we want to share with our closest friends, yet the more we share them, the less treasured and more spoiled they become. And so it is that to get away from it all, we must often steer down a gravel road and perhaps even take it until it is transformed into a dirt trail, one of those infamous "minimum maintenance roads." Then, when that runs into oblivion, we may find what we're looking for.

The find may be my special grouse covert, 80 acres of popple, fir, and birch interspersed with numerous tag-alder and prickly ash thickets. Traversing the entire area are a couple clover-sewn trails, each lined with dogwood and blackberry bushes. The nearest human habitation is over a mile away. The folks there own this piece and always guard it jealously during deer season, but they have no special affinity for grouse, so in October I hunt without any competition save that from goshawks, horned owls, and coyotes. I once took but five steps into these woods when an explosion of three grouse detonated from the brambles underfoot, catching me so off guard that my one desperation shot was hurled in utter futility at least 10 yards behind the last escaping bird. No wonder the ruffed grouse is the king of game-birds!

I know another gravel road that leads to a 500 acre marsh peppered with cattails and often surrounded by fields of corn and soybeans. There are other sloughs and lakes nearby but this one is special. It is tucked away in the very center of the section, mandating a healthy hike from the truck to the water's edge. The journey is a daunting one, laced with stubborn waist-high slough grass and gigantic pocket gopher mounds everywhere. Most hunters won't expend the time and energy to lug decoys, guns, shells, and waders that distance. But the slough holds ducks and geese, and they trade back and forth between this and other nearby sloughs.

Lord willing, some Saturday next fall, Mike and Mark and I will be out there once again, and by the time the eastern horizon glows pink, we will have our two dozen decoys perfectly placed. Hopefully mallards, woodies, teal, and wigeons will streak in from the big slough two miles south and they will make a couple passes overhead, carefully studying our spread. The boys and I will be decked out in full camo, and if I can keep our yellow Lab motionless on a muskrat mound, maybe the mallards will set their wings, extend those big orange feet, and come gliding into the blocks. I can already envision the rising sun shimmering off their iridescent green heads. Waterfowling! What a rush!

Then again, the gravel road we're on could wind through miles of Chippewa National Forest, with its majestic towering Norway and White Pines, until the path abruptly culminates in a 300 acre jewel of a bass lake. The lake rarely sees heavy pressure because there are many other, more accessible lakes in the vicinity. But it holds bass, lots of them, and big ones. The biggest largemouth of my life, a 23 inch bruiser over seven pounds, was caught and released here just a couple years ago, and on one notable guide trip, my customers and I caught and released 114 bass in one day. The water is clean and clear, the weedlines pronounced, and the bluegill population supports a magnificent largemouth fishery. Thank the Lord for isolated lakes!

It is a shame we have to spoil God's creation. With a burgeoning human population, more of whom are pursuing that "dream cabin" on a lake, it is becoming increasingly difficult to "get away from it all." That's what is appealing about gravel roads. I curse them, I look for alternate routes on the map; but as long as gravel roads exist, it likely means this particular corner of the planet receives little traffic. That suits me fine.

What a blessing to realize God has created people of such avocational diversity. An aunt of mine from a large Eastern city once visited us at our cabin and cut short her stay by two days. The days were too quiet and too boring; they made her nervous and uptight. Similarly, I've met North Dakotans who are uncomfortable if they cannot see the horizons; trees seem to hem them in. If everyone longed for quiet lakes, sprawling sloughs, or uninhabited woods as much as I do, such places would no longer exist. Thank God for large, noisy, smelly metropolises—and for all the people who choose to stay there.

May we always find gravel roads.

Psalm 23:

The Lord is my shepherd, I shall not be in want. He makes me lie down in green pastures, he leads me beside quiet waters, he restores my soul. He guides me in paths of righteousness for his name's sake.

Even though I walk through the valley of the shadow of death, I will fear no evil, for you are with me; your rod and your staff, they comfort me.

You prepare a table before me in the presence of my enemies. You anoint my head with oil; my cup overflows. Surely goodness and love will follow me all the days of my life, and I will dwell in the house of the Lord forever.

MALE BONDING

During the decade of the '90s, we heard a lot about male bonding. I guess a bunch of guys getting together without interference from the female persuasion was deemed a good, maybe even necessary thing. Of course, no one really knows what guys do at such gatherings, but I suspect it is considerably different from what girls do in a similar situation.

Contrary to the common belief held by feminists today, not all male bonding is characterized by beer, belching, brawling, and bragging. Some of the times I spend alone with sons Mike and Mark can accurately be described as male bonding experiences, and believe me, they are very positive and uplifting occasions.

For several years now, the boys and I have met in Dubuque, Iowa for the annual Iowa duck opener. There is nothing particularly magical about Dubuque, or Iowa for that matter, but Mark is in Michigan attending Calvin Seminary, while Mike and I continue to live in Minnesota. Six hundred miles separate us. Dubuque happens to be a midway point, representing a six hour drive for each of us. Furthermore, Minnesota's duck season generally doesn't open until around October 1, but Iowa offers an early season in mid-September. To someone for whom waterfowling is a passion, the decision to head south to Iowa to get a jump start on the duck season is a no-brainer. That is pretty much why the boys and I continue this tradition; besides, it is a good excuse for the three of us to get together and spend time doing what we enjoy most. There's that male bonding thing again.

My sons have always shown an unusual affinity for waterfowl, and I do mean "always." Mike went on his first "duck hunt" with me at age three or four. Obviously he didn't carry a gun; I doubt he could even *lift* one, but he accompanied me nevertheless. At the time, we were living in Northwest Iowa, a region renowned for its abundant pheasant population. Unfortunately, the area also lacks sloughs and marshes, so waterfowling is not a rich tradition there. I used to joke that a mallard flew through Northwest Iowa once in '78, but it was during the night, so I didn't get to see it. That may be a slight misrepresentation of the truth, but let's just say that the local sporting goods store didn't move a lot of duck decoys in the fall.

One evening after supper, I decided to walk a stretch of the Floyd River in the hopes of flushing a stray wood-duck. It was early fall, well before the pheasant season, and I had hunting fever. As usual, little Mikey wanted to go along with his dad, but his short, stubby legs were not suited for tramping through the underbrush along the river, so I opted instead to just "post" at a bend in the river and wait for sunset. Who knows, maybe some early migrant was in the vicinity and would come down the river at sunset. Mike and I picked a suitable spot on the river, and together we fashioned a make-shift blind out of tumbleweeds. Then we waited. I held my 12 gauge in one hand, and held Mikey's finger with my other hand. We visited and talked, and I tried answering all his questions. He seemed pretty proud of his good fortune at age four as he stood there on the riverbank with one of my old hunting caps perched on his head and a spare duck call dangling from his neck.

The sun was dipping below the trees, and the cool night air was beginning to seep in when I spotted them; coming straight at us, following the river, were three wood-ducks, boring in on us from about 300 yards away.

"Mike, don't move, don't say a word, here come three ducks!" At the command, Mike miraculously stood motionless, not uttering a sound. Ducks fly very fast, but the time it took those three woodies to close the gap between us seemed to take forever. My heart was thumping at this rare opportunity, and my palms began to sweat as little Mikey still gripped my finger. They were 70 yards away now, and in only a couple seconds they would be in range. Mike was playing his part to perfection; he must have sensed my urgency, for the little tyke wasn't moving a muscle. But that was before he actually spotted the three ducks. All of the sudden, he thrust his free hand into the air, pointed at the three birds and hollered, "There they are, Dad, I see them!"

I doubt there have ever been three more frightened wood-ducks, and as they instantly flared and clawed for altitude, leaving me no chance for a shot, I couldn't help but laugh aloud at Mikey's actions. I certainly couldn't fault him for this particular episode; his exuberant pride at spotting those three birds was so intense that I just had to laugh. But we never did eat much duck in Iowa.

That enthusiasm for ducks on the wing has not diminished in my sons' minds over the years, and that is why our Dubuque rendezvous last fall was anticipated for months. Many a phone call discussed such details as which motel to choose, what time we would arrive, how many shells we should take, who would pack the lunch, and a host of other matters. When the appointed Friday arrived, one last phone call was made to Mark to confirm that, yes, he was ready to leave. I drove to the Twin Cities, picked up Mike, and we headed southeast to meet Mark.

The trip itself was uneventful, though filled with talk of appropriate shotshells for pass-shooting, how bad the mosquitoes were going to be at dawn in this unusually warm weather, how high (or low) the water level would be, and anything else remotely involving waterfowl. Upon arriving in Dubuque, we made the disappointing discovery that our $29.95 motel room was indeed worth only $29.95. There is sometimes a fine line between frugality and Dutch stinginess, and at this particular time, we crossed that line. The back of my truck was only marginally less tidy than the room (and only marginally smaller, also), and had there been just two of us rather than three, we may have opted for the truck instead. We remarked that it was a good thing the women were not along. Sheri and Heather would have taken one step into that room and gingerly backed out, then I would have been the beneficiary of the "look" from Sheri.

The three of us talked and joked well into the morning hours, with the full realization we had to rise very soon in order to complete the 45 minute drive to the slough and be out in our blinds by daylight. Common sense dictated that we shut up and get a couple hours' sleep, but we hadn't seen each other for two months, and we were excited about the hunt, so common sense was not an option.

The 4 a.m. alarm startled all three of us awake, and given the "R" value of the insulation in our motel room walls, the alarm likely startled a few other residents, also. Still groggy from just two hours of fitful sleep, we downed a breakfast of powdered sugar donuts while hauling gear out to the truck.

For a couple hours that day and again the following morning, Mike and Mark and I crouched in the slough, waist deep in the dark, duckweed covered water, camouflaging ourselves behind scattered cattail clumps. There were some slow periods, but also several fast flurries, intermittent enough to keep us vigilant the entire time. The ducks came in from every possible direction, making shooting very challenging. There were abundant blown shots, plus many ducks that streaked through so low as to escape our "radar," but several ducks also folded into the water at our shots. It was a glorious way to spend a September weekend!

My fondest memory of that weekend duck hunt is not the eight ducks we each bagged. It is not the wave after wave of protected giant Canada geese that drifted over our heads in tempting gunshot range. It is not even the remarkable crossing shot I made on a drake mallard the first morning. Rather, it is what happened after we had called it quits the second day.

Tired, sweaty, wet and dirty, we had waded out of the slough and walked the railroad tracks back to where we had parked the truck. Soon we would split up and head home, Mark driving east while Mike and I headed back to Minnesota. Before we could do that, however, we had 12 more ducks to clean. Back at the truck we broke out the fillet knives and the ice chest. The fowl were promptly cleaned and tucked into the cooler, and we dried off the knives and scrubbed our hands clean in the moist grass. It had been a fantastic day and a half together. Plenty of ducks flew close, a few responded favorably to our calls, and the three of us "bonded"—once again. God had answered many prayers, both great and small. Many miles had been driven late at night—all safely. All three of us were in good health, even free from the common but nagging autumn head cold. We also all enjoyed periods of good shooting, not necessary in formulating a good hunt, but a positive bonus nevertheless. Overwhelming gratitude swept over us, and spontaneously, while standing in the shadows next to my truck, Mike suggested we bind our thoughts together and lift up a prayer of thanksgiving to God.

In a tight circle, we held hands, and in the quiet of a Sunday noon, with the pungent odor of slough gas all around us and the occasional raspy "quack, quack!" emanating from the marsh, Mike offered our gratitude heavenward. We were deeply struck with our good fortune, and were not unmindful of the fact that it was not accidental or even coincidental.

Life can be *so* good! God had freely rained on us His grace, and we had freely drunk it in. Memories are made at times like these, and we remembered with thankfulness that "all good things come from God's hand."

James 1:17, 18:

Every good and perfect gift is from above, coming down from the Father of the heavenly lights, who does not change like shifting shadows. He chose to give us birth through the word of truth, that we might be a kind of firstfruits of all he created.

Tate Publishing & *Enterprises*

Tate Publishing is committed to excellence in the publishing industry. Our staff of highly trained professionals, including editors, graphic designers, and marketing personnel, work together to produce the very finest books available. The company reflects the philosophy established by the founders, based on Psalms 68:11,

"THE LORD GAVE THE WORD AND GREAT WAS THE COMPANY OF THOSE WHO PUBLISHED IT."

If you would like further information, please call
1.888.361.9473
or visit our website
www.tatepublishing.com

Tate Publishing & *Enterprises*, LLC
127 E. Trade Center Terrace
Mustang, Oklahoma 73064 USA